W9-DET-048

Life!

ESSENTIALS FOR CHRISTIAN LIVING

JOAN HUNTER

Life! Essentials for Christian Living

© 2014 Joan Hunter

ISBN: 978-0-9829516-7-5

Published by Hunter Books
PO Box 411, Pinehurst, TX 77362 USA
HunterBooks@joanhunter.org
www.joanhunter.org

No part of this book may be reproduced, stored in a retrieval system or transmitted in any form or by any means – electronic, mechanical, photocopy, recording or any other – except for brief quotations, without permission in writing from the publisher.

Unless otherwise indicated, all Scripture is taken from the Holy Bible, New Living Translation (NLT), copyright © 1996, 2004, 2007 by Tyndale House Foundation. Used by permission of Tyndale House Publishers, Inc., Carol Stream, Illinois 60188. All rights reserved.

Scripture marked NKJV is taken from the New King James Version. Copyright © 1982 by Thomas Nelson, Inc. Used by permission. All rights reserved. Scripture marked NIV is from THE HOLY BIBLE, NEW INTERNATIONAL VERSION®, NIV® Copyright © 1973, 1978, 1984, 2011 by Biblica, Inc.™ Used by permission. All rights reserved worldwide. Scripture marked (AMP) is taken from the Amplified® Bible, Copyright © 1954, 1958, 1962, 1964, 1965, 1987 by The Lockman Foundation. Used by permission. www. Lockman.org. Scripture marked NASB is taken from the New American Standard Bible ®, Copyright © 1960, 1962, 1963, 1968, 1971, 1972, 1973, 1975, 1977 1995, by The Lockman Foundation. Used by permission. (www.Lockman.org). Scripture taken from The Message. Copyright © 1993, 1994, 1995, 1996, 2000, 2001, 2002. Used by permission of NavPress Publishing Group. Scripture marked ERV is taken from the Easy to Read Bible. Copyright ©2006 World Bible Translation Center, All rights reserved. Scripture marked KJV is taken from the King James Version. Public domain.

Cover design by Yvonne Parks at www.pearcreative.ca
Interior design by Katherine Lloyd, www.theDESKonline.com
Naida Trott RN, CWS, FCCWS, Ordained through Charles and Frances Hunter. Editor, Joan Hunter Ministries

Printed in the United States of America

Contents

FOREWORD

As a new believer in Christ, it is very important that you begin your new life with the right information and simple revelation of what the next steps in your new life should be. So many times what we learned in church or the things passed on by our parents, loved ones, pastors, and friends was not incorrect; it was just incomplete. Joan Hunter's book increases our understanding of how to begin to walk out the Christian life to ensure consistent spiritual growth.

As the Holy Spirit has brought you into relationship with God the Father through His Son, Jesus, the next call is for you to become a disciple of Jesus Christ. I think *LIFE!* is a must-have resource to help new believers become fully equipped and experience rapid immersion into their new life, family, and lifestyle as Christian.

Joan Hunter has prayerfully and carefully labored with the Holy Spirit from her heart to write this book. I know that as you read this book the Holy Spirit will enthusiastically meet you where you are and help you to become just like Jesus!

SEAN RANDALL, SENIOR PASTOR
W.A.R. Ministries
Ordained through Joan Hunter Ministries
www.pastorsean.org

INTRODUCTION

I Said The Prayer ... Now What?

Are you a new Christian? Did you recently speak the prayer of salvation?

Whether God led you down the aisle of a church or found you in a dark place, you have been introduced to your heavenly Father. By admitting you have not been a picture of perfection since the day you were born, you have taken the first step. Maybe you are going through a crisis in your life and have discovered that you don't have all the answers.

The Bible, God's Word, has answers you can trust. In fact, every answer you seek can be found within its pages in some form. The Bible is the authority to value and respect.

Most people know that Christianity is based on the Bible. As a new Christian, to sit down with God's Word can be somewhat intimidating. Some answers you are looking for may include:

Who will help me?

Where do I go to learn more?

Which translation of the Bible do I use?

Which church do I go to?

Can't I just watch church on TV or the Internet?

Do I have to read the Bible every day?

These and many other questions are answered in this book. I have attempted to answer the most common questions and situations new believers experience during this growth period. You can search for more at your leisure. Learning to find your answers within the Bible is a lesson in itself as you grow in your new Christian life. Most of the Scripture is taken from the New Living Translation because it is written in simpler English terms for ease of understanding. If a passage is not taken from the NLT, you will see the abbreviation of another translation after the Scripture reference.

Many of your old habits and friends will still appear, but they will undoubtedly change as you develop a new Christian family. You will find a different way of life as well as a new way of thinking. It is a new life. Your goals will change. Your language will change. Your personality will change. Your destiny has already changed. You are now on your way to spend eternity with your heavenly Father.

Just like anything new and different, there is a learning curve. Maybe you made your way to the altar years ago but never found direction for the next step on your journey. Perhaps Christians around you use words you don't understand, and you don't want to ask for a definition. You will discover the definition of many of these words or phrases as you read this book. Note that references or words related to God, Jesus, or the Holy Spirit will be capitalized in respect for Who He is.

I encourage you to start a journal to keep a record of how you progress and grow in the months and years ahead. It will be meaningful to you and your family in the years to come.

You are His reward and His unconditional love for you is too profound to measure because it has no end. God the Father set a vision of you before His Son as His reward for His work on earth. Now God will set before you a new vision for your life. You will face challenges, but you also have the opportunity to identify and build a life that is, in itself, a testimony of grace and love.

Enjoy!

SECTION ONE

RELATIONSHIP WITH GOD

SPIRITUAL BIRTH CERTIFICATE

This document is to announce the official

spiritual birthday of:

_____ ,

(Name)

Who has entered into the family of God

by accepting Jesus Christ as Lord and Savior,

On this _____ day of _____ in the year _____ ,

Through repentance from previous sins.

And now commits obedience in heart, mind, and soul to God.

Signature: _____

Witnessed by: _____

Presented by: _____

What Is the Family of God?

A celebration is in order! You have had a birthday, a spiritual birthday! You are a new creation with God as your Father. You have joined a new family with sisters and brothers all around the world. What fun you will have meeting them from this day forward!

You have been adopted into the family of God with all the rights of any other child. An exciting road is ahead of you as you discover all the blessings and love waiting for you. God is now your Father, and He is full of more love and compassion than any earthly father could even understand or express.

Some people have the impression that the Christian life is boring. Far from it! It is the most exciting life on the earth! The happiest, most content people on the earth are believers in the Lord Jesus Christ. Now you have joined us. Welcome!

> *For all who are led by the Spirit of God are children of God. So you have not received a spirit that makes you fearful slaves. Instead, you received God's Spirit when he adopted you as his own children. Now we call him, "Abba, Father."* (Romans 8:14–15)

> *This resurrection life you received from God is not a timid, grave-tending life. It's adventurously expectant, greeting God with a childlike "What's next, Papa?" God's Spirit touches our spirits and confirms who we really are. We know who he is, and we know who we are: Father and children. And we know we are going to get what's coming to us—an unbelievable inheritance! We go through exactly what Christ goes through. If we go through the hard times with him, then we're certainly going to go through the good times with him!* (Romans 8:15–17, MSG)

13

See how very much our Father loves us, for he calls us his children, and that is what we are! But the people who belong to this world don't recognize that we are God's children because they don't know him. Dear friends, we are already God's children, but he has not yet shown us what we will be like when Christ appears. But we do know that we will be like him, for we will see him as he really is. (1 John 3:1–2)

What Does It Mean to Be a Child of God?

Man was created by God, Who was and is the ultimate Father of all humankind. Those who accept Jesus are warmly welcomed into God's family. He truly became your spiritual Father when you committed your life to Him. As His child, your inheritance now includes all that He owns. You belong to Him. His Son, Jesus, is now your Brother as well as Lord.

For you are all children of God through faith in Christ Jesus. (Galatians 3:26)

So now Jesus and the ones he makes holy have the same Father. That is why Jesus is not ashamed to call them his brothers and sisters. (Hebrews 2:11)

Humans were initially created for relationship with their Creator, and that hasn't changed. God created the family in the first chapter of the Bible. When you join an earthly family, you laugh together, cry together, grow together, and love together through interaction, communication, and a very close relationship with one another. Your spiritual family is no different.

God will do this, for he is faithful to do what he says, and he has invited you into partnership with his Son, Jesus Christ our Lord. (1 Corinthians 1:9)

Because of Christ and our faith in him, we can now come boldly and confidently into God's presence. (Ephesians 3:12)

God drew you to His side because He loves you and wants a special family relationship with you. Yes, you! You can talk to Him any hour of the day or night. He is never too busy. He never has a headache. You can spiritually crawl up in His lap and feel His arms around you when you need some loving support. When life gets hard, He is always available to give you wise counsel and advice.

You aren't "saved" just to join a church, contribute to a building fund, help a missionary in China, or make goodies for the bake sale. Those may be a small segment of being a Christian, but hardly the most important part of your new life. The most vital and important experience of your new life is your intimate, very personal relationship with your Father God and Jesus Christ.

You are God's chosen. Do you understand? God chose you. He has watched and guided you throughout your life. He knew you before you took your first breath on the earth. You are His. He chose you for a special assignment, and it is up to you to find out why you were created and what He wants you to do.

I knew you before I formed you in your mother's womb before you were born I set you apart and appointed you as my prophet to the nations. (Jeremiah 1:5)

God's plan for your life is specifically designed for you and the gifts He placed within you. Everyone is given certain talents. What do you like to do? What excites you? What can you do for hours and never feel tired? What motivates you to get up in the morning and get moving? What do you love to talk about or study? All of the talents God has placed within you will play a part in what He has called you to do. He doesn't call everyone to be a missionary to a country on the other side of the world. Your present home and city have plenty of unsaved people who need to hear about Him. He will use you right where you are with the people you already know. If you have no musical talent, He will not direct you to sing or play in a band. Listen to Him. Be obedient. If He can trust you to do small things, He will then talk to you about more important assignments.

Do I Have to Pray Every Day?

Do you talk to your spouse daily? Do you speak to your children daily? Do you communicate with friends daily? God is your best friend forever. Why wouldn't you want to talk to Him numerous times a day?

A common picture of "prayer" shows someone alone in a corner of a church on their knees with their eyes closed and hands folded. Yes, this is an indication of deep, sincere prayer; however, prayer is so much more than that portrayal.

How do you pray? You open up your mouth and talk to God. Yes, just talk to Him! You don't have to use fancy King James English or any other proper wording. God understands whatever you say to Him. More than that, He understands your heart before you utter a sound. You can talk to Him about everything—your deepest hurts, hopes, desires, and dreams.

Many believe you can only talk to God while on your knees in church or by the side of your bed. Actually, you can talk to Him anywhere you happen to be at any time of the day or night. He is omnipresent (all around you at all times) and can hear your heart, your silent prayer, your whispers, and your normal voice. Life seems to bring occasions when you want to yell for help. He can certainly hear that as well.

His Spirit lives within you and never leaves you. That means you can talk to Him whenever you want or need to speak with Him. My friend's grandmother was known for "talking to herself" frequently. Many thought she was senile, but she had actually been to several Oral Roberts' meetings where she had learned to pray without ceasing; she was actually praying!

The Bible explains that the apostles didn't know how to pray. Jesus taught them the perfect prayer in the book of Matthew.

> *Our Father in heaven, Hallowed be Your name. Your king-dom come. Your will be done On earth as it is in heaven. Give us this day our daily bread. And forgive us our debts, As we forgive our debtors. And do not lead us into temptation, But deliver us from the evil one. For Yours is the kingdom and the power and the glory forever. Amen.* (Matthew 6:9–13, NKJV)

Spend some time studying the Lord's Prayer. It contains a wealth of information and wisdom. Numerous books have been written to explain the meaning of each sentence. Notice, it starts out praising God. This reminds whoever speaks these words that God is the One in charge of heaven and the earth. You are agreeing with His position and will.

Two words require a brief explanation: "debts" and "debtors." In today's world, a debt is usually money owed to someone else. A debtor is someone who owes you. In God's vocabulary, a debt is a sin. A debtor is someone who has done something wrong to you.

The New Living Translation of the Lord's Prayer actually says, *"and forgive us our sins, as we have forgiven those who sin against us."*

These are powerful words. God's forgiveness of your sins is dependent on your forgiveness for all the negative or bad things other people do to you. As you grow, you will learn more about unforgiveness, which can cause physical, emotional, and mental diseases. It can keep you vulnerable to the enemy and out of God's protection. It can also block your blessings.

What do you talk to God about? Everything. There is no subject that is off limits. He knows what you do every minute of every day. There are no secrets between you and God. He knows all the answers to questions you haven't even asked yet. He will give you the best possible advice in every situation. You just have to ask for His help before you do or say anything.

Prayer is not meant just for you to talk to God about your problems or situations. You can talk to Him about other people, with other people, or for other people and situations. Talking to Him should be as comfortable and easy as talking to your best friend because that is exactly what He is.

When someone wants to pray "for" you, they actually want to talk to God about you. Usually, this is a very good thing. Prayers to bless someone, give them wisdom and guidance, or heal them are all very common. To pray with someone else about a subject is very important also. Agreement in prayer is a very powerful tool.

I also tell you this: If two of you agree here on earth concerning anything you ask, my Father in heaven will do it for you. For where two or three gather together as my followers, I am there among them. (Matthew 18:19–20)

You may hear someone use the phrase, "lift someone up in prayer." This is another way of saying they are praying for that person. You symbolically lay that person or problem in your hand. Lift your hand to God to lay it at His feet or at the foot of the Cross.

Another way to say this is, "lay it at the Cross." When you spiritually/mentally "lay" something at the Cross, you are saying you believe God will handle the situation, and you are not going to worry about it any further.

It is difficult not to pick the problem up again and continue to worry about it or attempt to figure out the answer in your natural mind. You won't be the only one who does this. Often, a problem is laid at the Cross and picked up again many times until the only option is to allow God to solve the situation because there is absolutely nothing anyone can do in the natural.

Our ministry office gets prayer requests from people around the world via phone or email. Do long-distance prayers work? Oh, yes! God's Word has no boundaries. The power and anointing of His Word flows across the airways without a problem. There is no distance in the spirit realm . . . prayers and knowledge are not limited by miles, distance, or walls. Where two or three are gathered, He is there also.

You can "gather together" on a phone conversation as well as in person. A phone call is often the ideal method of contact because there are fewer distractions, privacy is maintained, and access is so readily available. His Word is "sent" many ways in modern society. You just have to open your heart and spirit to receive what is being sent to you.

When you were saved, you said what is called "The Sinner's Prayer." The exact words are not set in stone. Each prayer will use different words or phrases; however, there are certain things that have to be included. An example follows:

Father, I know that I have sinned. I ask you now to separate my sins from me and put them on the cross. I am truly sorry for what I have done in the past. Today, I turn from my sins and embrace all You have for me. I believe that Your

Son, Jesus Christ, died in my place to pay for my sins, was resurrected from the dead, and is alive forevermore. Jesus, I ask You to forgive me of my sins. I invite You to become the Lord of my life and to rule and reign in my heart from this day forward. I want to follow Your will for the rest of my life. Father, through Your Holy Spirit, lead me and guide me into ALL You have for me. In Jesus' name I pray. Amen.

Yes, you should be talking to Him every day. Actually, you should talk to Him frequently during your daily activities. Make it a habit to converse with Him and ask His advice often.

How Do I Hear God's Voice?

Does God talk to you? Yes, He does, and He would like to talk to you more. Our world is so noisy with so many demands on our time and attention, but God is a perfect gentleman and will not yell over the clamor of life.

God waits patiently for you. He wants you to realize He is the Source for all things. If you want peace, isolate yourself from the noise of the world. Find a quiet place where you can hear His still small voice. A quiet park or room is quite acceptable. Yes, God can talk to you anywhere; however, a place where you can focus on Him is best.

Prepare a private corner in your home where you can meet regularly with Him. Seek Him early in the morning or late at night when the family is sleeping. Focus your thoughts on Him. Sing praises to Him. Worship Him with a song. When you seek Him, you will find Him. God speaks in many ways. You may have a strong impression to pick up the Bible and read a certain passage. You may suddenly have ideas to solve a serious problem which you have never considered before.

His answers and His instructions always bring peace. He is not the author of confusion so don't accept any negative thoughts. He will instruct you. Yes, He may correct you but always so gently. Remember, God brings peace. Follow peace.

What Is a Revelation?

God has many ways to accomplish His will and purpose. Don't do anything not found in the Word. He will direct you with His Word, through His servants and church leaders (live or on TV / online), books, CDs, DVDs, or revelation. A revelation is knowing what God would do in a particular situation. Something is revealed to you. Perhaps an answer to a question you have been asking suddenly is right in front of you.

Sometimes a revelation is just for your use. However, God doesn't usually give you a truth to hide. It is to help others through their Christian journey. Only Jesus opens our eyes to the true meaning of the Word. He will show you what you need to do and what needs to change.

Who Can Help Me Learn?

God is your ultimate Teacher because you are now His child. You are part of His family, and He is a very good Father. He will guide your footsteps wherever you go and whatever you do. Ask for His help and listen for His leading. He will never leave you.

Just as I was with Moses, I will be with you. No one will be able to stop you all your life. I will not abandon you. I will never leave you. (Joshua 1:5, ERV)

21

"The mountains may disappear, and the hills may become dust, but my faithful love will never leave you. I will make peace with you, and it will never end." The Lord who loves you said this. (Isaiah 54:10, ERV)

For He Himself has said, "I will never leave you nor forsake you." (Hebrews 13:5b, NKJV)

Of course, you want someone more tangible to discuss things with and learn from. Pastors, preachers, and teachers are available in the local churches. Find a church that will assist you through these steps. There should be a class for new believers available.

If a Christian friend brought you to church or has encouraged you in the past, reach out to them with your questions. Most committed Christians have favorite books and teachers that helped them during their walk. Books, TV, CDs, DVDs, the Internet, and radio are also readily available today for continued learning and direction.

Where Do I Learn More?

As your hunger to learn grows, seek out seminars or conferences where you can soak in His Word through anointed praise, worship, and teaching by Christian leaders. Do some research. Find out what the speakers believe and who is sponsoring the meetings.

Most speakers and Christian organizations have a website with their statement of beliefs available. Ask your friends for recommendations. Where do they go? Who do they listen to?

Remember your leaders who taught you the word of God. Think of all the good that has come from their lives, and follow the example of their faith. Obey your spiritual leaders, and do what they say. Their work is to watch over your souls, and they are accountable to God. Give them reason to do this with joy and not with sorrow. (Hebrews 13:7, 17)

Keep in mind, this book is just the beginning steps along your Christian path. Every subject within these pages could be expanded into a book by itself. You can certainly follow up with your own research on any one aspect of Christianity and find numerous books written about it. Read and study; however, make sure everything you read is measured against the Word of God and not man's opinion.

Where Do I Find a Mentor?

During your walk, you will discover that certain people seem to "speak" to you more than others. Even though they don't know you, their messages seem to "read your mail." In other words, their teachings seem to answer your questions before you have spoken the words or thoughts.

These teachers may become your mentor through their teachings without any personal one-on-one conversation. Ideally, you will find a person who will spend personal time with you on a regular basis to answer your questions face-to-face or by telephone.

There is not just one place to find an earthly mentor. A pastor could be a good choice; however, many of them are too busy for much private time with individuals. Try a leader of a Bible study or organization. God will bring someone across your path. A mentor may be there to support you for a day, a month, a year, or a lifetime. You may have several mentors along the way. Be open and receptive for help in many areas.

What Is an "Accountability Partner," and Why Do I Need One?

Not everyone has an accountability partner, but as a new believer, it is a good idea. Two people agree to be accountable to each other for all areas of their behavior. With God's leading and guidance, two people pray together, talk things over, and seek God so that they can keep each other on the correct path. If one feels the other is not praying enough or seeking God appropriately, they can speak up and confront the other.

There is nothing legalistic or judgmental in the relationship. It is meant to help each person stay under the umbrella of God's protection and will. This partner can be a mentor or a very good Christian friend. Accountability partners should be of the same sex because all subjects and issues may be open to discussion.

Most interdenominational churches have accountability partners or mentors. These people are chosen because of their spiritual maturity, wisdom, integrity, and previous reputation. The church leadership and activities of the organization are "supervised," "overseen," or "approved" by those chosen. The church is accountable to these "mentors."

SECTION TWO

THE BIBLE

Why Is the Word Called the Good News?

The Good News is not a good story that you hear on radio or see on TV. Quite the opposite. The Good News is the salvation story through Jesus Christ leading to eternal life with Him in heaven. Usually, people are referring to the New Testament or perhaps just the Gospels of Matthew, Mark, Luke, and John. The word *gospel* means the good news of salvation, the story of Christ. The word is often interchanged with "Good News."

There is so much meaning and knowledge throughout the Bible, and it all points to Christ and is "good news" to Christians. Every time you pick up the Bible to read and learn, you will understand more and more about God's world. Every thought from His Word is a seed planted within your spirit. As it is watered and nurtured, your spirit will grow into what God wants you to be.

To make her holy and clean, washed by the cleansing of God's word. (Ephesians 5:26)

You must be in His Word to activate His blessings and rise to a higher level. The Word of God shows who Jesus is, God's plans for you and the world, and, basically, cleans up lives.

For I know the thoughts that I think toward you, says the Lord, thoughts of peace and not of evil, to give you a future and a hope. (Jeremiah 29:11, NKJV)

Which Bible Do I Use?

This is a very good question. Years ago, there was only one version of the Bible readily available, and the only decision necessary was to choose the size of the book. Today, there are dozens of versions. Your age, education, vision, language of choice, and level of

Christian growth all play a part. Bibles can be free, cost a few dollars, or be very fancy and expensive.

The King James Version is the most common Bible used through the ages. Because it is written in "King James' English," it can be challenging to understand. The Living Bible or Common English Bible would probably be easier for new believers. Many people end up with several versions until they decide on their favorite. Of course, children's Bibles are written at age appropriate levels. If English is your second language, you may want to try a children's Bible first and then advance to other versions as your understanding increases.

Visit your public library or local bookstore where you can look through several versions before purchasing your own personal Bible. The church where you were saved may have given you a free Bible. Use it until you find the version of God's Word that speaks to your heart.

When a scriptural reference is quoted, it is usually followed by the version of the Bible used. Often an abbreviation is used instead of the entire name. For instance, the King James Version is KJV; the New King James Version is NKJV; the Amplified is AMP; the New Living Translation is NLT; and the New International Version is NIV. There are so many versions available; you can research online if you find other abbreviations used in books or quotations.

How Can I Understand the Bible?

Do you find the Bible confusing? Most new believers do. Some books of the Bible do not seem to make sense to a new Christian. You will learn slowly but surely like everyone else did. Many will tell you to begin with the book of John in the New Testament, and, indeed, it is a good place to start.

John 3:16 sums up the salvation message in one paragraph, and it is a favorite verse of most believers. The Book of Psalms is also good. Most Christians know Psalm 23 because it paints such a beautiful picture of Jesus, the Shepherd, leading His sheep, the believers, through life.

> *For God so loved the world, that He gave His only begotten Son, that whoever believes in Him should not perish, but have everlasting life.* (John 3:16, KJV)

> *The Lord is my shepherd; I shall not want. He makes me to lie down in green pastures; He leads me beside the still waters. He restores my soul; He leads me in the paths of righteousness For His name's sake. Yea, though I walk through the valley of the shadow of death, I will fear no evil; For You are with me; Your rod and Your staff, they comfort me. You prepare a table before me in the presence of my enemies; You anoint my head with oil; My cup runs over. Surely goodness and mercy shall follow me All the days of my life; And I will dwell in the house of the Lord Forever.* (Psalm 23, NKJV)

Most importantly, before you start reading anything, ask God where He wants you to begin. Ask Him to open your understanding to His Word. Let Him guide you through the Bible. Very few people ever start with the first chapter of Genesis and read through the entire Bible to the last chapter of Revelation. That is a challenge for much later in your Christian walk.

The Bible is a book of life, a roadmap. It is the embodiment of God's instructions to us, His children. His Words are Spirit and Life to all who read and believe it. It is divided into two sections, the Old Testament and the New Testament, which are literally written contracts, or covenants, between God and His creation, us.

A covenant is a formal agreement between two parties, a very solemn promise to do or not do something specific. Many are familiar with the term "Last Will and Testament." The words "covenant" and "testament" are interchangeable. In God's vocabulary, His covenants include promises or agreements that are effective both during life on the earth and in heaven.

In the Old Testament, God's covenant with Abraham was sealed with a blood sacrifice; thus, it is often referred to as a "blood covenant." This was a very serious agreement in effect until the death of the parties involved. It can also follow through to the generations to come. The old covenant between God and His people required animal sacrifices (blood) for forgiveness of sins. Two signs of His covenant from the Old Testament are still apparent today—circumcision and the rainbow.

> *On that day the Lord made a covenant with Abram.*
> (Genesis 15:18, NIV)

> *The Lord our God made a covenant with us at Mount Sinai.*
> (Deuteronomy 5:2)

> *This is my covenant with you and your descendants after you,*
> *the covenant you are to keep: Every male among you shall*
> *be circumcised. You are to undergo circumcision, and it will*
> *be the sign of the covenant between me and you.* (Genesis
> 17:10–11, NIV)

> *When you came to Christ, you were "circumcised," but not by*
> *a physical procedure. It was a spiritual procedure-the cutting*
> *away of your sinful nature.* (Colossians 2:11)

> *I set My rainbow in the cloud, and it shall be for the sign*
> *of the covenant between Me and the earth.* (Genesis 9:13,
> NKJV)

The New Testament explains God's new covenant with man. The ultimate blood sacrifice for all humans for eternity is well-documented. God provided His own Son, Jesus, to die as a sacrifice for the sins of everyone who believes in Him.

In the same way, after the supper he took the cup, saying, "This cup is the new covenant in my blood, which is poured out for you." (Luke 22:20, NIV)

The Bible is filled with God's promises to His children. These promises are part of His covenant or contract with man. Promises are usually thought of as beneficial, fun, and beautiful. Most of His promises are indeed great and very desirable. Believers hang onto and often repeat His promises in all areas of life. You need to study these and know His promises are written specifically to you. (See Deuteronomy 28:2–14.)

People often forget that some of His promises are related to the opposite side of the coin. His promises often have a flipside to them. In other words, what will happen "if" His children are disobedient and rebellious? These promises are usually called "curses" because they are the negative; they are the consequences no one wants to experience. You must learn these also. (See Deuteronomy 28:15–68.)

Yes, God has rules. Parents have rules. The government has rules, better known as "laws." If you keep and obey the rules or laws, everything is good. If you disobey, there are consequences. This principle was first designed by God. Government authorities simply followed His example.

The rules of the country you live in are in effect whether you know them or not. It is your responsibility to learn what is expected of you and how to avoid negative consequences. The same goes for God's rules. Some unsaved people actually follow "good" principles and are blessed, not ever knowing that they are following God's laws without their knowledge. They may be wealthy and appear happy; however, without the saving knowledge of Jesus Christ, they are still lost and not going to heaven.

Part of the new believer's education is to learn what God wants, His rules of behavior, and what consequences to expect for disobedience. Once saved, a believer should concentrate on all the beautiful and wonderful blessings of God. No one dwells on the negative aspects or consequences of rebellion. However, just like living on the earth, you must be informed. Know both sides, the pros and cons. Learn to recognize what wise choices you should make in every situation.

Ask for God's understanding every time you open His Word.

[Blessings for the Lord's People] So the Lord must wait for you to come to him so he can show you his love and compassion. For the Lord is a faithful God. Blessed are those who wait for his help. (Isaiah 30:18)

Do I Have to Read the Bible Every Day?

If you had a special friend who wrote you a personal message every day of your life, would you read it? Of course, you would. You have a special connection with that friend who only wants the best for you and your life. A true friend is there during the good times as well as the bad. Regardless of your mistakes or falls, they stand by you, cheer you on, and, occasionally, a true friend will tell you when you are wrong and help you get back on track.

Your best friends in the whole existence of the world are your Father God, His Son, Jesus, and the Holy Spirit, the Trinity. Who else wants the very best for you every minute of every day of every year of your life? Why wouldn't you want a special message from

Him every day? His Word was written as a love letter to you with all the answers you will ever need.

No one will force you to read your Bible. If you love God and His Word, you will look forward to eating of His message daily and treasure His book above all others. Your spirit needs to be fed. It yearns for connection to your Creator.

What does "eating His Word" mean? Basically, you will read a portion of Scripture, think about it, consider how it will affect your life, taste it, and absorb it into your being where it will nourish your soul and make you stronger. You will take every promise personally, feel every word of encouragement down to your toes, and rejoice. His love will grow within you as you digest and utilize every morsel of His living Word. His Word is Life. Enjoy your dinner!

Taste and see that the Lord is good. Oh, the joys of those who take refuge in him! (Psalm 34:8)

For Your word has given me life. (Psalm 119:50b, NKJV)

It is the Spirit who gives life; the flesh profits nothing. The words that I speak to you are spirit, and they are life. (John 6:63, NKJV)

SECTION THREE

SALVATION

What is Salvation?

What actually happened when you got "saved" and said the prayer? It was not just an emotional reaction to a good speaker. It was God drawing you to His side. Read these amazing verses:

> *For God saved us and called us to live a holy life. He did this, not because we deserved it, but because that was his plan from before the beginning of time—to show us his grace through Christ Jesus. And now he has made all of this plain to us by the appearing of Christ Jesus, our Savior. He broke the power of death and illuminated the way to life and immortality through the Good News.* (2 Timothy 1:9–10)

> *But—"When God our Savior revealed his kindness and love, he saved us, not because of the righteous things we had done, but because of his mercy. He washed away our sins, giving us a new birth and new life through the Holy Spirit. He generously poured out the Spirit upon us through Jesus Christ our Savior."* (Titus 3:4–6)

> *All who came before me were thieves and robbers. But the true sheep did not listen to them. Yes, I am the gate. Those who come in through me will be saved. They will come and go freely and will find good pastures. The thief's purpose is to steal and kill and destroy. My purpose is to give them a rich and satisfying life. "I am the good shepherd. The good shepherd sacrifices his life for the sheep."* (John 10:8–11)

> *But the love of the Lord remains forever with those who fear him. His salvation extends to the children's children of those who are faithful to his covenant, of those who obey his commandments!* (Psalm 103:17-18)

For Jesus is the one referred to in the Scriptures, where it says, "The stone that you builders rejected has now become the cornerstone." There is salvation in no one else! God has given no other name under heaven by which we must be saved. (Acts 4:11–13)

For the grace of God has been revealed, bringing salvation to all people. And we are instructed to turn from godless living and sinful pleasures. We should live in this evil world with wisdom, righteousness, and devotion to God. (Titus 2:11–12)

What we do see is Jesus, who was given a position "a little lower than the angels"; and because he suffered death for us, he is now "crowned with glory and honor." Yes, by God's grace, Jesus tasted death for everyone. God, for whom and through whom everything was made, chose to bring many children into glory. And it was only right that he should make Jesus, through his suffering, a perfect leader, fit to bring them into their salvation. (Hebrews 2:9–10)

Even though Jesus was God's Son, he learned obedience from the things he suffered. In this way, God qualified him as a perfect High Priest, and he became the source of eternal salvation for all those who obey him. And God designated him to be a High Priest in the order of Melchizedek. (Hebrews 5:8–10)

You love him even though you have never seen him. Though you do not see him now, you trust him; and you rejoice with a glorious, inexpressible joy. The reward for trusting him will be the salvation of your souls. This salvation was something even the prophets wanted to know more about when they prophesied about this gracious salvation prepared for you. (1 Peter 1:8–10)

This is good and pleases God our Savior, who wants everyone
to be saved and to understand the truth. For there is only one
God and one Mediator who can reconcile God and human-
ity—the man Christ Jesus. (1 Timothy 2:3–5)

Throughout the Bible, God gave man explicit instructions for a successful life on the earth. Man's poor choices got him in trouble time after time. If God hadn't reached down to "save" His creation, man would have been destroyed long ago. Man did reach out for his Father on numerous occasions and begged for mercy.

God's mercy, grace, and favor seem endless. Earthly fathers would never have been so patient with their children's silly antics through the ages. Mercy encompasses compassion, kindness, and forgiveness. God certainly shows mercy towards His disobedient children. Man doesn't get what he deserves or none of us would still be alive.

His grace shows His love, mercy, kindness, and favor to man. It is often described as God's "unmerited favor." It truly is something we have not earned. It is not deserved. It is a gift from a forgiving Father who loves His children. You are His child.

God's law was given so that all people could see how sinful
they were. But as people sinned more and more, God's wonder-
ful grace became more abundant. So just as sin ruled over all
people and brought them to death, now God's wonderful grace
rules instead, giving us right standing with God and result-
ing in eternal life through Jesus Christ our Lord. (Romans
5:20–21)

For "Everyone who calls on the name of the Lord will be
saved." (Romans 10:13)

Sin is no longer your master, for you no longer live under the requirements of the law. Instead, you live under the freedom of God's grace. (Romans 6:14)

But there is a great difference between Adam's sin and God's gracious gift. For the sin of this one man, Adam, brought death to many. But even greater is God's wonderful grace and his gift of forgiveness to many through this other man, Jesus Christ. (Romans 5:15)

Because of his grace he declared us righteous and gave us confidence that we will inherit eternal life. (Titus 3:7)

So now there is no condemnation for those who belong to Christ Jesus. (Romans 8:1)

This High Priest of ours understands our weaknesses, for he faced all of the same testings we do, yet he did not sin. So let us come boldly to the throne of our gracious God. There we will receive his mercy, and we will find grace to help us when we need it most. (Hebrews 4:15–16)

But God is so rich in mercy, and he loved us so much, that even though we were dead because of our sins, he gave us life when he raised Christ from the dead. (It is only by God's grace that you have been saved!) For he raised us from the dead along with Christ and seated us with him in the heavenly realms because we are united with Christ Jesus. (Ephesians 2:4–6)

So God can point to us in all future ages as examples of the incredible wealth of his grace and kindness toward us, as shown in all he has done for us who are united with Christ

Jesus. God saved you by his grace when you believed. And you can't take credit for this; it is a gift from God. Salvation is not a reward for the good things we have done, so none of us can boast about it. (Ephesians 2:7–9)

And I am convinced that nothing can ever separate us from God's love. Neither death nor life, neither angels nor demons, neither our fears for today nor our worries about tomorrow— not even the powers of hell can separate us from God's love. No power in the sky above or in the earth below—indeed, nothing in all creation will ever be able to separate us from the love of God that is revealed in Christ Jesus our Lord. (Romans 8:38–39)

What Does It Mean to Be Born Again?

The phrase "born again" means "born from above." The term doesn't make much sense to the normal man. Even Nicodemus questioned Jesus in the Bible.

Jesus replied, "I tell you the truth, unless you are born again you cannot see the Kingdom of God." "What do you mean?" exclaimed Nicodemus. "How can an old man go back into his mother's womb and be born again?" Jesus replied, "I assure you, no one can enter the Kingdom of God without being born of water and the Spirit. Humans can reproduce only human life, but the Holy Spirit gives birth to spiritual life. So don't be surprised when I say, 'You must be born again.'" (John 3:3–7)

When you accepted Christ into your life by faith, He entered your heart to live through you. How does He do that? His Holy Spirit lives within you. Again, it is your choice to allow Christ to work through you. When you touch another person, it is Him touching through your hand. When you open your mouth to speak, you choose to allow Him to speak through you. You can function using the mind of Christ. All you have to do is ask Him to use you and then obey.

If you try to hang on to your life, you will lose it. But if you give up your life for my sake and for the sake of the Good News, you will save it. (Mark 8:35, AMP)

And so, dear brothers and sisters, I plead with you to give your bodies to God because of all he has done for you. Let them be a living and holy sacrifice—the kind he will find acceptable. This is truly the way to worship him. Don't copy the behavior and customs of this world, but let God transform you into a new person by changing the way you think. Then you will learn to know God's will for you, which is good and pleasing and perfect. (Romans 12:1–3)

My old self has been crucified with Christ. It is no longer I who live, but Christ lives in me. So I live in this earthly body by trusting in the Son of God, who loved me and gave himself for me. (Galatians 2:20)

A dead sacrifice can't do much to further God's kingdom. A living sacrifice can change the world! Isn't God marvelous? He gave His Son to the world to save man from sin. By Jesus' death and resurrection, He sends His Spirit to live within every believer forming His perfect body, the church—both you and I.

God makes you new and gives you a new heart, a new mind, and a new way of living. For God saved us and called us to live a holy life. He did this, not because we deserved it, but

*because that was his plan from before the beginning of time—
to show us his grace through Christ Jesus. And now he has
made all of this plain to us by the appearing of Christ Jesus,
our Savior. He broke the power of death and illuminated the
way to life and immortality through the Good News.*
(2 Timothy 1:9–10)

*But now we have been released from the law, for we died to it
and are no longer captive to its power. Now we can serve God,
not in the old way of obeying the letter of the law, but in the
new way of living in the Spirit.* (Romans 7:6)

"What Would Jesus Do?" (WWJD) became a common phrase
amongst Christians, especially the youth, in the last decade. It is a
very good habit to adopt into your young Christian life. Before acting or speaking, you should ask that question. If someone is yelling
at you, stop and ask yourself, "What would Jesus do in this situation?" If someone is mean or ugly to you, stop and ask the question.
Ask before you speak or act.

*Imitate God, therefore, in everything you do, because you are
his dear children.* (Ephesians 5:1)

Jesus replied in love, acted with love, and walked in love. You
will quickly find it is not easy to respond like Jesus in all situations.
Your flesh, your old habits, will arise. Your actions will show you
how well you are listening to His Spirit's still small voice. God is
Love, pure Love. God is a gentleman and won't force you to do
anything. You have to consciously make the choice to listen to His
voice and follow His principles or succumb to your previous habits
of the world (the enemy).

But we understand these things, for we have the mind of Christ.
(1 Corinthians 2:16b)

Renew your mind. The normal mind must hear things numerous times before it remembers and puts the thought into action. Left alone, the mind will fall back to its old way of thinking and direction. How many times does a parent have to remind a child to pick up their toys or shut the door or wash their hands before the child develops the habit? Countless times!

Our Father has to remind us to follow His Word also. Instead of going through the same lesson time after time, develop the habit of reading His Word on a regular basis to keep your thoughts focused on Him and His guidance. Renewing your mind could also be interpreted as keeping your focus on God and His Word. That is where your wisdom, strength, purpose, direction, and knowledge come from.

When you were saved and born again, you received the mind of Christ because He lives within you. When any situation arises, you can pause, plug in to Jesus, and ask, "What would You do in this situation, Jesus?" Think, speak, and act like God and miracles will happen. You were made in His image. When the enemy looks at you, he should see God's armor staring back at him.

But whenever someone turns to the Lord, the veil is taken away. For the Lord is the Spirit, and wherever the Spirit of the Lord is, there is freedom. So all of us who have had that veil removed can see and reflect the glory of the Lord. And the Lord—who is the Spirit—makes us more and more like him as we are changed into his glorious image. (2 Corinthians 3:16–18)

If the Good News we preach is hidden behind a veil, it is hidden only from people who are perishing. Satan, who is the god

of this world, has blinded the minds of those who don't believe.
They are unable to see the glorious light of the Good News.
They don't understand this message about the glory of Christ,
who is the exact likeness of God. (2 Corinthians 4:3–4)

Isn't it wonderful? God unveiled your eyes so you can truly understand all He has for you through Christ Jesus. No longer does Satan have you blinded. Once you accepted Jesus, He opened your eyes. Now you can see Truth.

I Grew Up in Church; Why Did I Have to "Get Saved"?

"My parents (and grandparents) were Christians. Doesn't that make me one?" No. "My father and grandfather were pastors, and I sang in the choir. Isn't that enough?" No. "I was baptized as a baby. Doesn't that mean I was saved?" No.

No one goes to heaven on the faith or belief of another person. Each individual has to come to God for themselves and no one else. Many have sat in church for centuries and never walked the aisle to ask Jesus into their heart or life. They have not enjoyed living in the fullness of Christ. One pastor freely says he was an evangelist who traveled with other well-known preachers "before he was saved." God used him even before he accepted Jesus. Following his true heart change, he is now a powerhouse for Christ.

Each and every human on the earth has to come to the Cross of Jesus Christ, repent for their sins, and accept Jesus into their heart. No exceptions. No free passes. No follow the leader to heaven. Each person is responsible for their own salvation. No one can force another. You had to make your own decision. You made the choice.

Of course, before the age of accountability, children are covered by God's grace and mercy. This includes those people with mental disabilities of all ages also. When they die, they will be welcomed into God's arms.

What Am I Saved From?

For the wages of sin is death, but the free gift of God is eternal life through Christ Jesus our Lord. (Romans 6:23)

Because man has a sinful nature, he is actually born in sin. What child is not selfish, wanting "mine?" They must be trained as to what is right and what is wrong. Influences on young children are varied in today's society. God has assigned Mom and Dad as the primary teachers of their children, but others pop in all too often. Playmates from the neighborhood, day care, relatives, school, church, babysitters, and the television all plant seeds into a young child's mind. Imperfect ideas of the world take root and grow into rebellious disobedient behavior while parents wonder, "Why?"

If children don't learn the principle of right and wrong from their earthly parents, spiritual leaders, teachers, and elders, who they can see and feel, how can they ever know and respect the laws of God, Who they can't see? Children must be taught God's Word and how to understand His world. That responsibility belongs to the children's parents, not to the school, government, or church.

All actions have a reaction, a basic law of science. It is also a law of God. If you obey God, blessings will be your reward. If you disobey, there are consequences. Until you accept Jesus, your journey is directed at hell and destruction. Your destiny is death.

When you are saved, you are literally saved from an eternity in hell separated from your heavenly Father. Some say the prayer on their deathbed and sneak into heaven at the last minute. Thank God, they got saved! But what a wonderful life they missed!

What Is Sin?

A simple definition of sin is "missing the mark." Wikipedia explains that "sin is the act of violating God's will" or "anything that violates the ideal relationship between an individual and God."[1] Another dictionary says it is a "transgression of divine law" or "willful or deliberate violation of some religious or moral principle."[2] All those are included, but I believe it actually goes further than those definitions. It also includes not following God's instructions, which is a form of rebellion.

For all have sinned and fall short of the glory of God.
(Romans 3:23, NIV)

Therefore, just as through one man sin entered the world, and death through sin, and so death spread to all men, because all sinned. (Romans 5:12, NASB)

Sin was once avoided like the plague, and sinners—those who committed outward sin—were shunned or stoned. Today, sin has become so commonplace; it barely gets a shrug of the shoulders. Since everybody is doing it, somehow it has become part of everyday life and is ignored as nothing serious to be concerned about. Everyone has heard the phrase "a little white lie." A lie is a lie, whatever the "color," and is sin in God's eyes.

Sin is universal, and perhaps this is just one reason why the term is so frequently ignored. So many are sinning so frequently that it has become a normal way of life to them! It has become acceptable

---

1   "Sin," Wikipedia, http://en.wikipedia.org/wiki/Sin. Used with permission under the Creative Commons Attribution-ShareAlike 3.0 Unported License.
2   sin. Dictionary.com. Dictionary.com Unabridged. Random House, Inc. http://dictionary.reference.com/browse/sin (accessed: January 06, 2014).

because everybody is doing it! People have given up the goal to be perfect, to be more like Christ.

Everyone who sins is breaking God's law, for all sin is contrary to the law of God. (1 John 3:4)

Scripture has several definitions that describe sin. Trespasses and sin in the Old and New Testament include "deviating from the right way, path, or law; to fail to live up to an accepted standard." Sin is the failure to do what God wants us to do. Essentially, it is disobedience to His perfect will. God tells you to show love to the man on the street corner. You "don't want to" and walk the other direction. Your disobedience is sin.

And you He made alive who were dead in trespasses and sins. (Ephesians 2:1, NKJV)

Christianity is a way of living. It covers every facet of life. Following God's plan, you are truly alive and growing towards perfection. Not following God means you are sliding backwards towards a sinful life. The main idea of sin is failure. You sin when you fail to live up to the standards of life that God established and revealed through His prophets, apostles, and Jesus Christ. Sin is not confined to your conduct. It can be buried within your heart.

To the pure all things are pure, but to those who are defiled and unbelieving, nothing is pure; but both their minds and their consciences are defiled. (Titus 1:15, ESV)

Everyone has committed sin. No one is perfect. Everyone misses the mark, every day. So you have to repent daily for the things you should have done, things you did in error, or thoughts that you should have ignored or rebuked.

> *But I say, anyone who even looks at a woman with lust has*
> *already committed adultery with her in his heart.*
> (Matthew 5:28)

The driving force of sin comes from Satan, God's archenemy. He will do anything to separate man from God. His sole purpose is to destroy God's creation and drag man to hell. Since sin does separate us from God, sin is the primary weapon of Satan.

The depiction of an ugly creature in a red suit with a tail and carrying a pitchfork is from someone's imagination. Anyone would run from such a creature. The enemy comes in with subtle suggestions of deception, hate, anger, fear, and numerous other ways to draw you away from God. The Bible describes him as beautiful and full of light. He originated in heaven as an angel and was then cast out of heaven to the earth because of his own rebellion, pride, and jealousy. He entices and lies. Anything bad, evil, or chaotic comes from him.

Remember that peace is a gift from God, and chaos comes from Satan. You choose. Which do you want in your life?

Where Did Sin Come From?

God created the earth and everything in it. Because God wanted a relationship, He created man in His own image and breathed life into him. This first human was called Adam; he walked on earth thousands of years ago. Man needed more so God formed a woman from Adam's rib. He gave them the perfect place, the Garden of Eden, to live in. Together, they set out to populate the earth.

Along with the gift of life, God gave them free will, the power to choose because He didn't want puppets to blindly obey His every word. God wanted children, a family to live with Him, talk to Him, and worship Him, by choice out of love. It wasn't long before man and woman slipped off the right road and messed up God's blueprint for a perfect life. Listening to the enemy, they allowed Satan to influence their decisions and their fellowship with God. They opened the door for sin to enter the earth. Adam and Eve have been blamed through the ages for their mistake.

Years of disobedience followed. Through Moses, God gave man the rules of the road along with numerous other instructions about life on the earth. (See Exodus 20; Deuteronomy 5 and 28.) Satan got busy with his confusion and deception. Soon the beautiful world designed by the Father was seriously swamped with sin on all sides.

Every sin committed has a consequence, a penalty that has to be paid. In the Old Testament, animal blood sacrifices were the common payment for sins. Only a perfect specimen was ever acceptable. Throughout the Old Testament, there are examples of the sins of people and what God required to renew their relationship with their Creator.

The Ten Commandments, as well as the other scriptural rules for life, were given to show man how imperfect he was. Without rules to measure growth or behavior, no one knew where they stood. God told the people, wrote the rules in stone, and enforced punishments for disobedience. Man was stubborn.

God's heart ached at the misbehavior and rebellion of His creation. He wanted a relationship with man; however, a human couldn't stand before God covered with sin. How frustrated God must have been with man, how disappointed.

God knew man wasn't going to be perfect. From the beginning, He knew He would provide an eternal sacrifice in the form of His Son, Jesus. Only with the perfect sacrifice could man be reconnected and redeemed back to God.

What Negative Things Does Sin Do to Us and Others?

The first time you lie about something, you may feel a bit uncomfortable. As each lie comes out of your mouth, your conscience adjusts. Each lie, or sin, makes the next one a bit easier. Over time, lying becomes normal behavior. Sin is addictive like a drug. As the addiction becomes stronger, truth disappears. This happens with any wrong behavior. The first sin usually occurs as a child. Maybe no one corrected you so you continued the deception into adulthood. Taking something belonging to another becomes easier with each theft. Your God conscience is ignored as you become overtaken with sin after sin.

God gave you free will when you were born. You have to make the correct choice with every action. Maybe you failed because of weakness or curiosity. Recognize the failure and repent. Ask God to forgive you before an addiction makes the behavior a necessity in your life and your will has been destroyed.

The deceitfulness of sin! It seduces and entices. Sin promises pleasure, contentment, and fulfillment, which are very short-lived. Its deceitfulness is the very reason why it has addictive qualities. In the end, sin brings nothing but grief, pain, and heartache.

But there is another power within me that is at war with my mind. This power makes me a slave to the sin that is still within me. (Romans 7:23)

So I am not the one doing wrong; it is sin living in me that does it. (Romans 7:17)

Most assuredly, I say to you, whoever commits sin is a slave of sin. And a slave does not abide in the house forever, but a son abides forever. (John 8:34–35, NKJV)

And do not present your members as instruments of unrighteousness to sin, but present yourselves to God as being alive from the dead and your members as instruments of righteousness to God. For sin shall not have dominion over you, for you are not under law but under grace. (Romans 6:13–14, NKJV)

Be careful then, dear brothers and sisters. Make sure that your own hearts are not evil and unbelieving, turning you away from the living God. You must warn each other every day, while it is still "today," so that none of you will be deceived by sin and hardened against God. For if we are faithful to the end, trusting God just as firmly as when we first believed, we will share in all that belongs to Christ. (Hebrews 3:12–14)

"He who overcomes shall inherit all things, and I will be his God and he shall be My son." (Revelation 21:7, NKJV)

It is obvious that overcoming is a priority in a Christian's life. God doesn't expect you to do something that He didn't prepare you to do. He has given you the power and the tools to fight the enemy and be totally victorious. You will overcome the enemy, share in Christ's riches in Glory, and live with your Father forever just as the Scriptures teach. Sin will not have dominion over you. You just have to learn how to fight with God's weapons.

Paul wrote to the Ephesians about "spiritual wickedness," and to the Romans about sinful natures.

For we do not wrestle against flesh and blood, but against principalities, against powers, against the rulers of the darkness of this age, against spiritual hosts of wickedness in the heavenly places. (Ephesians 6:12, NKJV)

For the sinful nature is always hostile to God. It never did obey God's laws, and it never will. That's why those who are still under the control of their sinful nature can never please God.
(Romans 8:7–8)

First John teaches that those who have overcome the enemy are strong with the Word of God living within them. He continues to say you are not to *love* the world, its lusts, or *pride*.

Do not love this world nor the things it offers you, for when you love the world, you do not have the love of the Father in you. For the world offers only a craving for physical pleasure, a craving for everything we see, and pride in our achievements and posses-sions. These are not from the Father, but are from this world.
(1 John 2:15–16)

You must overcome Satan, his demons, and their evil influence. You must overcome your fleshly, human nature. Some say you must also overcome the world; however, the world's influence ultimately comes from Satan. Following peace, love, and truth, you can stay in God's will. You can do the right thing. An overcomer is victorious over sin! God doesn't ask you to do anything without preparing you for the assignment. He knows you can succeed!

Don't let evil conquer you, but conquer evil by doing good.
(Romans 12:21)

Anyone who meets a testing challenge head-on and manages to stick it out is mighty fortunate. For such persons loyally in love with God, the reward is life and more life. Don't let anyone under pressure to give in to evil say, "God is trying to trip me up." God is impervious to evil, and puts evil in no one's way. The temptation to give in to evil comes from us and only us.

We have no one to blame but the leering, seducing flare-up of our own lust. Lust gets pregnant, and has a baby: sin! Sin grows up to adulthood, and becomes a real killer. (James 1:13–15, MSG)

Sexual desire is a very common area where self-denial can be difficult for many. Indiscretions, infidelity, and extramarital affairs plague the church as well as the world. The first occurrence may bring guilt. The second, third, or fourth dulls the conscience. Since the world's opinion of free love without the sanctity of marriage is so open, such behavior is ignored. In the world, having multiple partners is common, but it is sin in God's eyes.

As soon as you are tempted, you must deny yourself the wrong desire. Jesus asks you to practice self-denial in your actions even before you do them. The enemy will tempt you in the area of your weakness. If you have never stolen anything before, you won't start now. However, if it was a problem in the past, you will be tempted to pick up something that doesn't belong to you. You will think, "No one will know." But God does.

I say then: Walk in the Spirit, and you shall not fulfill the lust of the flesh. For the flesh lusts against the Spirit, and the Spirit against the flesh; and these are contrary to one another, so that you do not do the things that you wish. But if you are led by the Spirit, you are not under the law. Now the works of the flesh are evident, which are: adultery, fornication, uncleanness, lewdness, idolatry, sorcery, hatred, contentions, jealousies, outbursts of wrath, selfish ambitions, dissensions, heresies, envy, murders, drunkenness, revelries, and the like; of which I tell you beforehand, just as I also told you in time past, that those who practice such things will not inherit the kingdom of God. (Galatians 5:15–23, NKJV)

*The Lord is slow to anger, abounding in love and forgiving sin
and rebellion. Yet he does not leave the guilty unpunished; he
punishes the children for the sin of the parents to the third and
fourth generation.* (Numbers 14:18, NIV)

That one verse of Scripture should make you sit up and take
notice. What you do today will affect your children to the third
and fourth generations that follow. Do you want your children and
grandchildren to suffer the consequences of your rebellious behavior or sin? Certainly not!

God's punishment means something different than man's definition. He doesn't cause discord and pain. However, His deliverance
from the enemy won't occur until He is invited to intervene. For
example, a spirit of divorce, murder, or anger is allowed to enter a
person's life. That is passed through to the next generation and the
next and the next until it is broken through repentance, ministry,
and prayer.

One act of rebellion spreads widely through your family, friends,
and co-workers. It affects everyone around you. In contrast, one act
of kindness or love also spreads the same way. What you plant into
your life or the life of someone else will grow into a harvest. If you
don't like what is growing around you, you need to consider making
a change in what you are planting. The "spirit" you allow into your
life will multiply and affect everything around you. Are you inviting
the spirits of fear, anger, hate, and rebellion from the enemy? Or are
you inviting God's spiritual gifts of love, joy, peace, and patience?

What Does It Mean to Clean House?

*I will give them an undivided heart and put a new spirit in
them; I will remove from them their heart of stone and give
them a heart of flesh.* (Ezekiel 11:19, NIV)

55

When you got saved, you asked God to forgive all the sins you committed. You gave God your heart and opened the door for Jesus to live in you forever. God washed you and gave you a new heart. You are brand new. Every bad thing you did before is gone. God has forgotten all the junk you were involved in. He holds nothing against you. Your slate is clean.

For his unfailing love toward those who fear him is as great as the height of the heavens above the earth. He has removed our sins as far from us as the east is from the west. The Lord is like a father to his children, tender and compassionate to those who fear him. (Psalm 103:11–13)

You have been "born again." You are a new creation committed to God, your heavenly Father. You have turned your life over to Him and have chosen to follow Him and His Word. All decisions of your past have made you what you are today, a new person in Christ Jesus.

This means that anyone who belongs to Christ has become a new person. The old life is gone; a new life has begun! (2 Corinthians 5:17)

The crown of life is a crown of righteousness, and righteousness can be defined simply as "right doing." An *overcomer* is victorious over sin and walks in His righteousness!

Blessed is the man who endures temptation; for when he has been approved, he will receive the crown of life which the Lord has promised to those who love Him. Let no one say when he is tempted, "I am tempted by God"; for God cannot be tempted by evil, nor does He Himself tempt anyone. But each one is tempted when he is drawn away by his own desires and enticed. Then, when desire has conceived, it gives birth to sin; and sin, when it is full-grown, brings forth death. (James 1:12–15; NKJV)

Do not be overcome by evil, but overcome evil with good. (Romans 12:21, NKJV)

Appetite, material goods, worldly ambitions, personal prestige, and sexual desires are very common areas where self-denial is tough for many. Lying, cheating, stealing, and gossiping are on the list also.

Since no one is perfect, what do you do when you mess up? Run towards God in faith to repent and start again. Never run away from your Father in fear. Learn from your mistakes, and never dwell on them. Remember your past life only in relationship to what God has done for you.

Reading all of this about sin and the penalties may bring up another question or two: "I've done a lot of things in the past. How do I get good enough for God? How can I be holy and acceptable to God? Don't I have to clean myself up before going to church? How can I ever be good enough?"

Part of the Good News is that God already knows you aren't perfect and holy. God sees you through His Son's eyes. When you ask for forgiveness (and we all do on a daily basis) and have faith in Jesus Christ, God erases your sin and welcomes you into His arms as if you were as holy as Jesus.

Jesus was the only perfect man that walked the earth. He made the way, He cleared the path, and He opened the door to the throne room for you by paying for everything you have done in the past or will do in the future.

Picture yourself walking through a shower of the bright red blood of Jesus Christ pouring over your black and evil sinful body. As you emerge on the other side, you are as pure and white as new fallen snow. It doesn't make sense in the natural mind; however, it is a reality in God's world.

With every difficult situation, temptation or test, remember, you know the end of the book . . . YOU WIN!

God does not tempt you, Satan does. Satan wants you to fall, to sin, and to turn your back on God. God may test you. He wants you to willingly choose His way to a victorious life. What is a test? In natural life, it shows us how we are doing on a specific subject. Tests in school aren't fun; however, they do show us our progress. The same is true in God's school.

The first time you have to confront, and say "no" to, a bad habit may be a challenge. The second time is easier. Each time the habit tries to take over, it gets easier to avoid. Maybe you aren't faced with it for months. Suddenly, it pops up again. What do you do? Give in and go back to it? Or laugh at it and stay victorious? Laugh. Loudly! It was a test, and you won!

Someone may ask you if you have cleaned your house. No, they haven't peeked in your windows or checked for dust on the windowsill. That is a physical cleaning process. As a Christian, you will want to embark upon a spiritual cleaning. Anything in your home that is not of God needs to be removed. A good friend of mine had astrology symbols and books, cult statues, and Masonic literature in their home. Her husband wore demonic jewelry and had pornography hidden in a closet.

Clean your house. Check your library for anything demonic. Don't claim you have it for research or information. You can go to the Internet or the library to research any subject in the world. Don't keep it in your home. What kind of music did you listen to before salvation? Much of the world's music is not fit to play in a church; thus, it is not appropriate to play in your home either.

If you don't want Jesus to see what is hidden in your home, get rid of it! Jesus lives inside of you and sees whatever you see. God already knows what you have done in the past and has forgiven you for your involvement. Get rid of any temptation to return to that garbage from the enemy! I don't care if the item was a valuable present from your parents or a dear friend! Your spiritual life is much more valuable than trash from the enemy!

Ask God what needs to be removed from your home. He will lead you to the items that are affecting the spiritual health of your home and your family. Once those items are gone, you can progress to praying over your home. Anoint areas of your home with oil if you wish. Pray over the oil or ask your pastor or mentor to pray over the oil before you use it.

How many supposedly innocent items creep into your home? The enemy has an open door through the Internet today. Nudity, pornography, demonic images, and information can "pop up" on your screen at anytime. Be aware that these things do affect the spiritual atmosphere of your home. Pray over gifts that enter your home.

Wise words satisfy like a good meal; the right words bring satisfaction. The tongue can bring death or life; those who love to talk will reap the consequences. (Proverbs 18:20–21)

You must also examine your words. Did you have a very "colorful" vocabulary? Habits can be hard to break. God can help you. Think before you speak. If you wouldn't say those words to your pastor, don't open your mouth! Can you imagine Jesus speaking those words? He lives in you. You may be the only Jesus they see. What the world sees is you. Do you represent Him well?

Don't use foul or abusive language. Let everything you say be good and helpful, so that your words will be an encouragement to those who hear them. And do not bring sorrow to God's Holy Spirit by the way you live. Remember, he has identified you as his own, guaranteeing that you will be saved on the day of redemption. Get rid of all bitterness, rage, anger, harsh words, and slander, as well as all types of evil behavior. Instead, be kind to each other, tenderhearted, forgiving one another, just as God through Christ has forgiven you. (Ephesians 4:29–32)

Dear brothers and sisters, when troubles come your way, consider it an opportunity for great joy. For you know that when your faith is tested, your endurance has a chance to grow. So let it grow, for when your endurance is fully developed, you will be perfect and complete, needing nothing. (James 1:2–4)

Accept the tests and trials because they will come. Share in His life. Jesus went through more than any other man before or since. You will never be asked to endure anything like He went through. Tests show you where you are because God already knows. He shows you how you are doing and whether you are going forward or backward.

If you think you are standing strong, be careful not to fall. The temptations in your life are no different from what others experience. And God is faithful. He will not allow the temptation to be more than you can stand. When you are tempted he will show you a way out so that you can endure. (1 Corinthians 10:12–14)

God doesn't leave you defenseless. He does send help in the form of Christian friends, mentors, and teachers to help you. He planned both your offensive and defensive weapons. You have the mind of Christ and have already been instructed on renewing your mind daily. In addition, and most importantly, He sends His Holy Spirit, the Comforter, to guide you through life from the first day you were saved. He is also called your Advocate, your Helper.

Instead, let the Spirit renew your thoughts and attitudes. (Ephesians 4:23)

But the Helper, the Holy Spirit, whom the Father will send in My name, He will teach you all things, and bring to your remembrance all things that I said to you. (John 14:26, NKJV)

Your true friends will change. With God as top priority in your life, you will want to talk about Him and what is happening in your life. Your old friends may not want to hear anything you want to say. Your interests in common have changed. They want to party, go to happy hour, and participate in other enticements of the world. You need new friends. Seek out people who believe as you do. Surround yourself with quality Christians who can help you, answer your questions, and support you during your battles with the enemy. Stay connected with His family.

Oh, the joys of those who do not follow the advice of the wicked, or stand around with sinners, or join in with mockers. But they delight in the law of the Lord, meditating on it day and night. They are like trees planted along the riverbank, bearing fruit each season. Their leaves never wither, and they prosper in all they do. (Psalm 1:1–3)

What Is Righteousness?

The word "righteousness" means "right standing with God." It is an attribute of God Himself. In very simple terms, righteousness is "doing the right thing." BibleStudyTools.com explains righteousness in the following manner:

God the Father is righteous (just); Jesus Christ his Son is the Righteous (Just) One; the Father through the Son and in the Spirit gives the gift of righteousness (justice) to repentant sinners for salvation; such believing sinners are declared righteous (just) by the Father through the Son, are made righteous (just) by the Holy Spirit working in them, and will be wholly righteous (just) in the age to come. They are and will be righteous because they are in a covenant relation with the living God, who is the God of all grace and mercy and who will bring to completion what he has begun in them by declaring them righteous for Christ's sake.[1]

Only God, Jesus, and the Holy Spirit are truly righteous (doing the correct thing) 100 percent of the time. Christians are righteous only through Christ Jesus by the Holy Spirit. Christians attempt to become like Christ with His attributes that include righteousness, or doing the right thing all the time. Man's righteousness fluctuates greatly because man is not perfect and must be reconciled back to the Father frequently. But, through Christ, our righteousness, or "right standing to the Father," is always assured.

Clearly, God's promise to give the whole earth to Abraham and his descendants was based not on his obedience to God's law, but on a right relationship with God that comes by faith. (See Romans 4:13.)

---

1 Righteousness, Bible Study Tools, www.biblestudytools.com/dictionaries/bakers-evangelical-dictionary/righteousness.html, taken from *Baker's Evangelical Dictionary of Biblical Theology*. Edited by Walter A. Elwell Copyright © 1996 by Walter A. Elwell. Published by Baker Books, a division of Baker Book House Company, Grand Rapids, Michigan USA.

Therefore, since we have been made right in God's sight by faith, we have peace with God because of what Jesus Christ our Lord has done for us. (Romans 5:1)

So now we can rejoice in our wonderful new relationship with God because our Lord Jesus Christ has made us friends of God. (Romans 5:11)

And the result of God's gracious gift is very different from the result of that one man's sin. For Adam's sin led to condemnation, but God's free gift leads to our being made right with God, even though we are guilty of many sins. For the sin of this one man, Adam, caused death to rule over many. But even greater is God's wonderful grace and his gift of righteousness, for all who receive it will live in triumph over sin and death through this one man, Jesus Christ. (Romans 5:16–17)

Yes, Adam's one sin brings condemnation for everyone, but Christ's one act of righteousness brings a right relationship with God and new life for everyone. (Romans 5:18)

There is none righteous, no, not one. (Romans 3:10, NKJV)

With the Lord's authority I say this: Live no longer as the Gentiles do, for they are hopelessly confused. Their minds are full of darkness; they wander far from the life God gives because they have closed their minds and hardened their hearts against him. They have no sense of shame. They live for lustful pleasure and eagerly practice every kind of impurity. But that isn't what you learned about Christ. Since you have heard about Jesus and have learned the truth that comes from him, throw off your old sinful nature and your former way of life, which is corrupted by lust and deception. Instead, let the Spirit renew your thoughts and attitudes. Put on your new nature, created to be like God truly righteous and holy. (Ephesians 4:17–24)

Putting on a new nature is not something you physically do; it is something you are as a child of God. By faith, you are saved. By faith, you ask and receive forgiveness from your Father. By faith, you are a new man. By faith, you can walk into His presence as His child, pure and holy, totally reconciled to your Father.

What Is Reconciliation?

Reconciliation is the act of reconciling. *Webster's New World College Dictionary* defines the word "reconcile" as the following:

> to make friendly again or win over to a friendly attitude; to settle (a quarrel, difference, etc.); to make (arguments, ideas, texts, accounts, etc.) consistent, compatible, etc.; bring into harmony; to make content, submissive, or acquiescent to; to become reconciled to one's lot.[1]

Christians discuss man's reconciliation with God because God can't be in the presence of sin. When man chooses to sin, he chooses to separate himself from God. Something must be done before man can return to God's holy presence.

In the Old Testament, animal sacrifices were necessary to erase the wrong doing of His children. Often the priests offered these sacrifices for the people or the entire country. Following Christ's sacrificial death, animal sacrifices were no longer necessary. Since then,

---

1 Webster's New World College Dictionary Copyright © 2010 by Wiley Publishing, Inc., Cleveland, Ohio. Used by arrangement with John Wiley & Sons, Inc. www.yourdictionary.com/reconcile.

each individual has to ask God for forgiveness, to repent for sin. By doing so, reconciliation is accomplished and His children can once again enter His Presence.

> *For if when we were enemies we were reconciled to God through the death of His Son, much more, having been reconciled, we shall be saved by His life. And not only that, but we also rejoice in God through our Lord Jesus Christ, through whom we have now received the reconciliation.* (Romans 5:10–12, NKJV)

> *This means that anyone who belongs to Christ has become a new person. The old life is gone; a new life has begun! And all of this is a gift from God, who brought us back to himself through Christ. And God has given us this task of reconciling people to him. For God was in Christ, reconciling the world to himself, no longer counting people's sins against them. And he gave us this wonderful message of reconciliation.* (2 Corinthians 5:17–19)

What Is Baptism?

Baptism is a very important rite (or formal ceremony or practice) of the church. New believers are encouraged to get baptized. Is it necessary for salvation? No, but it is a very public display of your faith and commitment to God from this day forward.

> *Therefore go and make disciples of all nations, baptizing them in the name of the Father and of the Son and of the Holy Spirit.* (Matthew 28:19, NIV)

For you were buried with Christ when you were baptized. And with him you were raised to a new life because you trusted the mighty power of God, who raised Christ from the dead. (Colossians 2:11–12)

Baptism is described as an example of death because man cannot live underwater. The old man symbolically dies when the person is immersed in the water. A new man arises out of the water to take a breath of fresh air, which starts his new life.

Once, it was thought that baptism was necessary for salvation, so babies were sprinkled with water on their forehead. Some churches still practice infant baptism; however, it has become infant dedication for others. Baptism with immersion, then, is done later when the person is capable of making a personal commitment to Christ. If a person is incapable of being immersed, such as the elderly or sick, sprinkling is still acceptable.

We were therefore buried with Him through baptism into death in order that, just as Christ was raised from the dead through the glory of the Father, we too may live a new life. (Romans 6:4, NIV)

Peter replied, "Each of you must turn from your sins and turn to God, and be baptized in the name of Jesus Christ for the forgiveness of your sins. Then you will receive the gift of the Holy Spirit." Those who believed what Peter said were baptized and added to the church--about three thousand in all. (Acts 2:38, 41)

John the Baptist baptized Jesus before Jesus started His ministry. By participation in baptism, you identify with Jesus and what He went through to give you salvation. It is a public confession of an inner experience. In baptism, you stand before witnesses confessing your sin and identifying yourself as a follower of the Lord Jesus Christ. Baptism paints a picture of Christ.

My old self has been crucified with Christ. It is no longer I who live, but Christ lives in me. So I live in this earthly body by trusting in the Son of God, who loved me and gave himself for me. (Galatians 2:20)

For we died and were buried with Christ by baptism. And just as Christ was raised from the dead by the glorious power of the Father, now we also may live new lives. Since we have been united with him in his death, we will also be raised to life as he was. (Romans 6:4–5)

And that water is a picture of baptism, which now saves you, not by removing dirt from your body, but as a response to God from a clean conscience. It is effective because of the resurrection of Jesus Christ. (1 Peter 3:21)

But you were cleansed; you were made holy; you were made right with God by calling on the name of the Lord Jesus Christ and by the Spirit of our God. (1 Corinthians 6:11)

Perhaps you were baptized as a baby. Being baptized by immersion now that you better understand your faith is not a problem. Many people have been baptized by immersion more than once. As an example, several of our ministry's team who went to Israel a few years ago chose to be baptized again in the Jordan River where Jesus was baptized. Being baptized is a decision between you and God.

SECTION FOUR

THE EXPRESSION
OF GOD

What Is the Trinity?

Taken from a Latin word meaning "three are one," the word "trinity" means the same in Christianity. However, it is used specifically to describe Father God, His Son Jesus Christ, and the Holy Spirit. These three entities of the Godhead work, think, and act as one Being, even though they each have different functions. God is the supreme Being, the heavenly Father; He is both the Creator and the Ruler of the universe. He is Omnipotent (unlimited power), Omniscient (unlimited knowledge), and Omnipresent (present everywhere at the same time).

Jesus, God's Son, was sent to the earth to die a sacrificial death to reconcile sinful man back to the Father. Christ means the "Anointed One." He is the central figure of Christianity. In fact, the term "Christian" means to be "Christ-like." As a Christian, you believe in Jesus Christ as the Son of God and Savior of the world. He was born of a virgin, He worked miracles while on this earth, and He was crucified. Following His death on the Cross and resurrection from the dead, He arose to sit at the right hand of the Father, where He intercedes for us daily. The only way to reach the Father is through His Son. Without Jesus, you cannot be saved or ever legitimately enter the Father's presence.

The Holy Spirit, also known as the Holy Ghost, is the third person of the Trinity. References to the Holy Spirit are found throughout the Bible, starting in Genesis 1:2. Before Jesus' ascension into heaven, the Spirit would come upon a person for a short time and for a specific reason. In the New Testament, the Holy Spirit planted God's DNA into Mary at Jesus' conception. He descended upon Jesus just after His baptism. When Jesus returned to heaven, He sent the Holy Spirit to actually live within all believers. He brings many godly attributes into our lives, including what are called the fruit and the gifts of the Spirit. These are activated by the baptism of the Holy Spirit.

What Is the Baptism of the Holy Spirit?

Next to salvation, the baptism of the Holy Spirit is probably the most important experience of the believer. Yes, you receive the Holy Spirit at salvation, or conversion; however, it is a separate experience to be immersed in the fullness of the Holy Spirit. Jesus needed the Holy Spirit to effectively minister in His day. You also need it today. John the Baptist first announced Jesus at His baptism.

I baptize with water those who repent of their sins and turn to God. But someone is coming soon who is greater than I am—so much greater that I'm not worthy even to be his slave and carry his sandals. He will baptize you with the Holy Spirit and with fire. (Matthew 3:11)

Then John testified, "I saw the Holy Spirit descending like a dove from heaven and resting upon him. I didn't know he was the one, but when God sent me to baptize with water, he told me, 'The one on whom you see the Spirit descend and rest is the one who will baptize with the Holy Spirit.' I saw this happen to Jesus, so I testify that he is the Chosen One of God." (John 1:32–34)

After his baptism, as Jesus came up out of the water, the heavens were opened and he saw the Spirit of God descending like a dove and settling on him. And a voice from heaven said, "This is my dearly loved Son, who brings me great joy." (Matthew 3:16–17)

A person can get saved and filled with the Holy Spirit at the same time; however, often there are two distinct experiences. Many have to seek God and ask for the Holy Spirit's baptism before the

Father gives them what they are looking for. If you haven't received the evidence of the Holy Spirit yet, ask.

> *So if you sinful people know how to give good gifts to your children, how much more will your heavenly Father give the Holy Spirit to those who ask him.* (Luke 11:13)

> *John baptized with water, but in just a few days you will be baptized with the Holy Spirit . . . ."But you will receive power when the Holy Spirit comes upon you. And you will be my witnesses, telling people about me everywhere—in Jerusalem, throughout Judea, in Samaria, and to the ends of the earth."* (Acts 1:5, 8)

Occasionally, flames of fire are seen in services where the Holy Spirit is moving. Baptism with fire can also mean the Holy Spirit is burning the garbage out of your life and is renewing a fiery hot desire for more of God within your heart.

> *Suddenly, there was a sound from heaven like the roaring of a mighty windstorm, and it filled the house where they were sitting. Then, what looked like flames or tongues of fire appeared and settled on each of them. And everyone present was filled with the Holy Spirit and began speaking in other languages, as the Holy Spirit gave them this ability.* (Acts 2:2–4)

> *Peter replied, "Each of you must repent of your sins and turn to God, and be baptized in the name of Jesus Christ for the forgiveness of your sins. Then you will receive the gift of the Holy Spirit. This promise is to you, and to your children, and even to the Gentiles—all who have been called by the Lord our God."* (Acts 2:38–39)

God doesn't give the Holy Spirit to anyone lightly. Along with this powerful gift comes a responsibility to use it wisely and well. The Holy Spirit brings fruit and gifts into the life of the believer who welcomes Him. If you have been called by God, you are eligible to receive the fullness of the Holy Spirit. Once you have received the Holy Spirit, you are "Spirit-filled."

Believers receive the Holy Spirit with evidence of speaking in tongues in many ways and at different places, and they can describe unique experiences. Some may receive Him at a meeting with hundreds of others at the same time. Another may be driving down the road in their car. Another might start talking in tongues in a bathtub full of bubbles. One may receive when hands are laid on them, while the other is simply reading their Bible or praying.

Again, God is no respecter of persons. He will give whenever and wherever He wants.

And God has given us his Spirit as proof that we live in him and he in us. (1 John 4:13)

We are witnesses of these things and so is the Holy Spirit, who is given by God to those who obey him. (Acts 5:32)

Then Peter and John laid their hands upon these believers, and they received the Holy Spirit. (Acts 8:17)

Then Peter replied, "I see very clearly that God shows no favoritism. In every nation he accepts those who fear him and do what is right." (Acts 10:34–35)

When the Spirit of truth comes, he will guide you into all truth. He will not speak on his own but will tell you what he has heard. He will tell you about the future. He will bring me glory by telling you whatever he receives from me. (John 16:13–14)

What Is the Fruit of the Spirit?

For a good tree does not bear bad fruit, nor does a bad tree bear good fruit. (Luke 6:43, NKJV)

But the fruit of the Spirit is love, joy, peace, longsuffering, kindness, goodness, faithfulness, gentleness, self-control. Against such there is no law. (Galatians 5:22–23, NKJV)

And this hope will not lead to disappointment. For we know how dearly God loves us, because he has given us the Holy Spirit to fill our hearts with his love. (Romans 5:5)

Prove by the way you live that you have repented of your sins and turned to God. (Matthew 3:8)

As with anything planted or grown, there is seedtime and harvest. The fruit of the Spirit is no different. It would be so nice to instantly show the world all the beautiful things God creates within you. Alas, your human ways don't necessarily become perfect instantly. You will work to develop these godly characteristics.

One thing is sure, however. God does change lives. Have you ever seen a drastic improvement in someone's personality? Chances are, God has gotten hold of them and is developing positive changes from inside out. Often, even a person's appearance changes. They look years younger, have a spring in their step, and a smile on their face.

Expect changes. These changes confirm that a person has truly committed their life to Christ and is allowing God to make them a "new creation." Words can be cheap. A person can say they believe but are still doing the things they have always done. If no fruit (godly characteristics) is showing, the validity of their salvation experience may be in question.

Do you walk in the fruit of the Spirit? Do you show others supernatural love? Do you have the joy of God in your heart regardless of the surrounding circumstances? Does peace follow you through the storms of life?

LOVE

God is Love. He is pure Love. He loves His children, His creation, so much that He gave His only Son as a sacrifice to save man from sin. You are to show the same kind of love to others through your actions, your words, and your life.

> *Love is patient and kind. Love is not jealous or boastful or proud or rude. It does not demand its own way. It is not irritable, and it keeps no record of being wronged. It does not rejoice about injustice but rejoices whenever the truth wins out. Love never gives up, never loses faith, is always hopeful, and endures through every circumstance.* (1 Corinthians 13:4–7)

Love God:

> *But anyone who does not love does not know God, for God is love.* (1 John 4:8)

> *And now, Israel, what does the Lord your God require of you? He requires only that you fear the Lord your God, and live in a way that pleases him, and love him and serve him with all your heart and soul.* (Deuteronomy 10:12)

Those who accept my commandments and obey them are the ones who love me. And because they love me, my Father will love them. And I will love them and reveal myself to each of them. (John 14:21)

Love Others:

But I lavish unfailing love for a thousand generations on those who love me and obey my commands. (Exodus 20:6)

Do not seek revenge or bear a grudge against a fellow Israelite, but love your neighbor as yourself. I am the Lord. (Leviticus 19:18)

Honor your father and mother. Love your neighbor as yourself. (Matthew 19:19)

So now I am giving you a new commandment: Love each other. Just as I have loved you, you should love each other. (John 13:34)

Love Brings Blessings:

If you carefully obey all the commands I am giving you today, and if you love the Lord your God and serve him with all your heart and soul, then he will send the rains in their proper seasons—the early and late rains—so you can bring in your harvests of grain, new wine, and olive oil. (Deuteronomy 11:13–14)

It is useless for you to work so hard from early morning until late at night, anxiously working for food to eat; for God gives rest to his loved ones. (Psalm 127:2)

God Never Fails:

For your unfailing love is as high as the heavens. Your faithfulness reaches to the clouds. (Psalm 57:10)

But you, O Lord, are a God of compassion and mercy, slow to get angry and filled with unfailing love and faithfulness. (Psalm 86:15)

Love is Protection to You and Your Children:

For you bless the godly, O Lord; you surround them with your shield of love. (Psalm 5:12)

The descendants of those who obey him will inherit the land, and those who love him will live there in safety. (Psalm 69:36)

The Lord says, "I will rescue those who love me. I will protect those who trust in my name." (Psalm 91:14)

But the love of the Lord remains forever with those who fear him. His salvation extends to the children's children. (Psalm 103:17)

No, O people, the Lord has told you what is good, and this is what he requires of you: to do what is right, to love mercy, and to walk humbly with your God. (Micah 6:8)

And we know that God causes everything to work together for the good of those who love God and are called according to his purpose for them. (Romans 8:28)

That is what the Scriptures mean when they say, "No eye has seen, no ear has heard, and no mind has imagined what God has prepared for those who love him." (1 Corinthians 2:9)

Always be humble and gentle. Be patient with each other, making allowance for each other's faults because of your love. (Ephesians 4:2)

JOY

The Joy of the Lord is unexplainable happiness. In the midst of crisis, joy can take over and reign supreme because you know the end of the Book. Often, His joy is the only thing that gets you through trying times. But His joy is wonderful. It lives deep down in your soul. It was planted there when Jesus was invited into your life. Nothing or no one can take it from you. You hang onto it for dear life.

Oh, the joys of those who trust the Lord, who have no confidence in the proud or in those who worship idols. (Psalm 40:4)

Joyful are those who obey his laws and search for him with all their hearts. (Psalm 119:2)

And so, my children, listen to me, for all who follow my ways are joyful. Listen to my instruction and be wise. Don't ignore it. Joyful are those who listen to me, watching for me daily

*at my gates, waiting for me outside my home! For whoever
finds me finds life and receives favor from the Lord.* (Proverbs
8:32–36)

For the joy of the Lord is your strength! (Nehemiah 8:10)

PATIENCE

Patience is probably a better word for longsuffering. The willingness
to wait patiently is proof of trust. Man wants things to manifest
immediately when God says, "Wait for my perfect timing." Can you
operate with kindness and goodness in all situations? Are you true
to your word? Are you faithful to your commitments and beliefs
regardless of the opposition? Do you allow Jesus to work through
you with gentleness and self-control as you deal with the world?

But a man of understanding holds his peace. (Proverbs
11:12b, NKJV)

*And the peace of God, which surpasses all understanding,
will guard your hearts and minds through Christ Jesus.*
(Philippians 4:7, NKJV)

*For God has not given us a spirit of fear and timidity, but of
power, love, and self-discipline.* (2 Timothy 1:7)

*May God, who gives this patience and encouragement, help
you live in complete harmony with each other, as is fitting for
followers of Christ Jesus.* (Romans 15:5)

We prove ourselves by our purity, our understanding, our patience, our kindness, by the Holy Spirit within us, and by our sincere love. (2 Corinthians 6:6)

PEACE

Peace. What a wonderful word! However, even having peace continuously would not be good for you. Challenges help you to grow. Still, peace is a fruit of the Spirit and needs to be understood.

God's peace paints a different picture than that of the world. Peace of the world means no one is fighting. God's peace says, "All is well," even in the midst of a battle. What is the difference? God's peace in your heart keeps you calm because you know the end of the book. Chaos can surround you, and, yet, you can stay calm and think with the clear mind of Christ. You know Who the Victor is. You make decisions based on what God wants you to do. No fighting. No bickering. No fists or nasty words. Just calm peace.

Those who love your instructions have great peace and do not stumble. (Psalm 119:165)

Nasty words and behavior breeds more of the same. God's calmness and a soft answer breed more of the same. Which do you prefer? I hope that you want the peaceful calmness of God to fill your life on a daily basis.

To sum up the fruit of the Spirit, ask yourself this question: *Do you respond and act like Jesus would in every situation?*

Most Christians have to repent for wrong attitudes daily. With Jesus' Spirit living within, you should be walking in the fruit of Jesus' Spirit every day and every minute just as God directs. When you miss the mark, you will find yourself asking for God's mercy and grace to forgive you and help you to do better in the future. Forgiveness for the little things is just as important as the big offenses.

Don't be misled—you cannot mock the justice of God. You will always harvest what you plant. Those who live only to satisfy their own sinful nature will harvest decay and death from that sinful nature. But those who live to please the Spirit will harvest everlasting life from the Spirit. So let's not get tired of doing what is good. At just the right time we will reap a harvest of blessing if we don't give up. (Galatians 6:7-9)

FAITH

Without faith, no one can please God. In fact, without faith, no one would even believe in Him.

This Good News tells us how God makes us right in his sight. This is accomplished from start to finish by faith. As the Scriptures say, "It is through faith that a righteous person has life." (Romans 1:17)

Enter his gates with thanksgiving; go into his courts with praise. Give thanks to him and praise his name. For the Lord is good. His unfailing love continues forever, and his faithfulness continues to each generation. (Psalm 100:4–5)

Great is his faithfulness; his mercies begin afresh each morning. (Lamentations 3:23)

You can pray for anything, and if you have faith, you will receive it. (Matthew 21:22)

Then Jesus said to the disciples, "Have faith in God."
(Mark 11:22)

He made no distinction between us and them, for he cleansed their hearts through faith. (Acts 15:9)

This Good News tells us how God makes us right in his sight. This is accomplished from start to finish by faith. As the Scriptures say, "It is through faith that a righteous person has life." (Romans 1:17)

So faith comes from hearing, that is, hearing the Good News about Christ. (Romans 10:17)

Be on guard. Stand firm in the faith. Be courageous. Be strong. And do everything with love. (1 Corinthians 16:13–14)

And it is impossible to please God without faith. Anyone who wants to come to him must believe that God exists and that he rewards those who sincerely seek him. (Hebrews 11:6)

So you see, we are shown to be right with God by what we do, not by faith alone. (James 2:24)

Just as the body is dead without breath, so also faith is dead without good works. (James 2:26)

Such a prayer offered in faith will heal the sick, and the Lord will make you well. And if you have committed any sins, you will be forgiven. (James 5:15)

Keep in mind, each fruit of the Spirit that you plant (or give to another) is a seed which multiplies and returns to you as a harvest. If you want more love in your life, give more love to others. If you want others to be more patient with you, exercise more patience when you deal with others.

Often you will hear about seedtime and harvest when talking about money or tithing. The principle can be applied to more than what finances you choose to give to God. It applies also to what you give to others. Share a smile, and you will get many in return. Share a frown, and you will reap a frown. What you plant will grow.

But now is the time to get rid of anger, rage, malicious behavior, slander, and dirty language. Don't lie to each other, for you have stripped off your old sinful nature and all its wicked deeds. Put on your new nature, and be renewed as you learn to know your Creator and become like him. (Colossians 3:8–10)

The seed that fell on good soil represents those who truly hear and understand God's word and produce a harvest of thirty, sixty, or even a hundred times as much as had been planted!" (Matthew 13:23)

What Are the Gifts of the Spirit?

Do not neglect your gift, which was given you through prophecy when the body of elders laid their hands on you. (1 Timothy 4:14, NIV)

But it was to us that God revealed these things by his Spirit. For his Spirit searches out everything and shows us God's deep secrets. No one can know a person's thoughts except that

person's own spirit, and no one can know God's thoughts except God's own Spirit. And we have received God's Spirit (not the world's spirit), so we can know the wonderful things God has freely given us. When we tell you these things, we do not use words that come from human wisdom. Instead, we speak words given to us by the Spirit, using the Spirit's words to explain spiritual truths. But people who aren't spiritual can't receive these truths from God's Spirit. It all sounds foolish to them and they can't understand it, for only those who are spiritual can understand what the Spirit means. Those who are spiritual can evaluate all things, but they themselves cannot be evaluated by others. For, "Who can know the Lord's thoughts? Who knows enough to teach him?" But we understand these things, for we have the mind of Christ.
(1 Corinthians 2:10-16)

There are different kinds of spiritual gifts, but the same Spirit is the source of them all. (1 Corinthians 12:4)

And God confirmed the message by giving signs and wonders and various miracles and gifts of the Holy Spirit whenever he chose. (Hebrews 2:4)

God has given each of you a gift from his great variety of spiritual gifts. Use them well to serve one another. (1 Peter 4:10)

What Gifts Are Given to the Church?

Now these are the gifts Christ gave to the church: the apostles, the prophets, the evangelists, and the pastors and teachers. Their responsibility is to equip God's people to do his work and build up the church, the body of Christ. (Ephesians 4:11–12)

Not even Jesus Christ chose to preach or teach to all the people Himself. He called twelve men to travel with Him and learn during His three short years of ministry on earth. After Jesus' death, His eleven disciples spread the Good News to the known world. They could not be everywhere. The work was too much for them alone, and they trained others to continue the spread of the gospel.

Just like any organization, there are offices filled by men or women depending on their expertise. In this case, their specialty depends on the gifts they have received from God. Each position has qualifications and responsibilities. Each position is a supernatural gift from God to His children.

No one person has all the answers. No one person has all the talents. Each person in the body of Christ has an important part of the whole. You might hear three teachings on a particular Scripture, and they are all different. That is because the three teachers have been given different insights into that subject, and, yes, they have all heard from God.

Now we see things imperfectly, like puzzling reflections in a mirror, but then we will see everything with perfect clarity. All that I know now is partial and incomplete, but then I will know everything completely, just as God now knows me completely. (1 Corinthians 13: 9–10, NKJV)

These offices or gifts are also known as the five-fold ministry.

APOSTLES

An apostle plants new churches, supervises growth, and mentors pastors. They can actually operate in all the positions of the five-fold ministry as God needs them. Apostles may be closely associated with a church but usually are traveling between the groups they oversee. It is a position truly given by God to a mature believer who has proven themselves through years of study, integrity in ministry, and faithfulness to the cause of Christ by spreading His pure gospel to the world. An apostle has a heart to develop and equip the body of Christ.

The apostle is a foundational role. They are humble and often in the background. They work with courage and the heart of a servant. Wanting to empower others, they teach and train. Often they experience much spiritual warfare as they push the boundaries of Christianity into hostile territory.

PROPHETS

Prophets seek God for new revelations and prophesy. Their messages predict the future based on divine revelation from God. They are set into the body of Christ to help in the area of spiritual correction for the corporate church. Prophets do not take the place of you seeking and hearing directly from God. Look to God for direction, not a prophet.

PASTORS

Pastors can be the leader of a church group, they can function as a spiritual adviser or mentor, and they will often teach their congregation and minister one-on-one to their members. They may be called ministers or preachers. They will teach and minister to a few or many, with a tender and compassionate heart. They have often been described as a shepherd because they take care of the flock, or congregation. Pastors are more involved with the intimate details of the congregation such as who is sick, who is in the hospital, who is having difficulties, and who needs extra ministry or prayer. Without a true compassionate heart of God, a man of God should not be in the role of pastor. They spend lots of time crying with the hurting, counseling the confused, and rejoicing over the miracles. They are very sensitive to the emotional state of those around them.

TEACHERS

Teachers are good sources of instruction on the Bible. They may have a primary focus such as Jewish history, the end times, faith, healing, or prosperity. You want to take notes as they release their insights on Scripture. They often appear to be a wealth of knowledge about God's Word. Indeed, what they pour out on the body of Christ is the result of thousands of hours of study and prayer behind the scenes.

You may notice they have a few points to focus on with Scripture or other references. Maybe all the points start with the same letter of the alphabet such as prophet, prophecy, pride, or profession. Their instruction may be given in multiple parts or a series with each part building on the last session. You will learn almost without realizing it because they will use colorful examples, diagrams, or visual aids to stimulate your memory.

EVANGELISTS

The evangelist travels with a primary message of salvation. Years ago, they were described as "hell-fire and damnation" preachers who scared you into heaven with their vivid descriptions of hell. Billy

Graham is the best-known evangelist of today. He has won multiplied thousands to the Lord through his extensive years of ministry.

Some operate in only one gift such as teaching, while others may operate in all of the gifts or positions depending on the call of God on their life and the job He has assigned them at the moment.

> *Here are some of the parts God has appointed for the church:*
> *first are apostles, second are prophets, third are teachers, then*
> *those who do miracles, those who have the gift of healing,*
> *those who can help others, those who have the gift of leader-*
> *ship, those who speak in unknown languages.* (1 Corinthians
> 12:28)

You can see there are gifts or positions other than the Five-Fold Ministry. You have an important assignment to the body of Christ. God has and will always give you the ability to fulfill that assignment. Part of that ability is known as an anointing.

What Is an Anointing?

This term is usually used in conjunction with religious ceremonies. It means someone or something is being set apart for God's service. Some, like in biblical times, use special anointing oil, which is applied on the head, forehead, or feet, during the ceremony. An official installation of someone into a particular office or position may use anointing oil. The oil, however, is not a necessary element.

Special anointing services are held today, but often there is little ceremonial process. It is a very sacred, personal event especially when the anointing passes from one believer to another. First of all, God is the One Who chooses you, sets you apart, and truly anoints you.

> *Now He who establishes us with you in Christ and has*
> *anointed us is God.* (2 Corinthians 1:21, NKJV)

Anointing is evident throughout the Bible to set someone apart from the rest. Leaders, kings, and priests were anointed into their office often using large amounts of oil; it was poured over their heads and allowed to run down their garments and onto the floor.

For thousands of years, dead bodies were often prepared for burial using special (and often very expensive) anointing oil. Jesus experienced this type of anointing before His burial in the gospel of Mark.

She has done what she could and has anointed my body for burial ahead of time. (Mark 14:8)

Jesus Christ actually means "Jesus, the Anointed One." He truly was set apart by His Father as a very unique spotless Lamb who would become the ultimate sacrifice for our sin. He is, was, and will always be our Messiah, Redeemer, Advocate, Brother, Son, Shepherd, High Priest, King, Lord, and Prince of Peace. He is the Word, and He is our best friend forever.

Today, the anointing can include God choosing and setting someone apart for a special gift or assignment. When a message particularly touches you, you may feel the supernatural power of God in the room. You may hear a comment, "That was such an anointed message." To a person sensitive to the Spirit of God, the anointing is almost tangible as if you could reach out and touch it.

Often, the anointing falls over a congregation during the praise and worship service. People are saved without an invitation, some are healed without hands-on ministry, and some will be set free. This is truly God working amongst His believers.

One person has the anointing, set apart with a special gifting, to teach. Another may have that special anointing to lay hands on the sick. There is not just one type of anointing; it is given and manifests as part of the Holy Spirit's presence in your life.

The Spirit of the Lord God is upon Me, Because the Lord has anointed Me To preach good tidings to the poor; He has sent Me to heal the brokenhearted, To proclaim liberty to the captives, And the opening of the prison to those who are bound.
(Isaiah 61:1, NKJV)

For me, the anointing for healing passed from my parents, Charles and Frances Hunter. They operated under a great anointing during their years in ministry. I have been told I have the anointing of both of them, which I treasure and will respect forever. It is such a gift from God, which I received gladly.

Without God's anointing, I can do nothing. With Him, I can preach the Good News, heal the sick, and free the captives. That is exactly what I have been doing, and I intend to keep on that same anointed path for the rest of my earthly life.

Remain in me, and I will remain in you. For a branch cannot produce fruit if it is severed from the vine, and you cannot be fruitful unless you remain in me. Yes, I am the vine; you are the branches. Those who remain in me, and I in them, will produce much fruit. For apart from me you can do nothing.
(John 15:4–5)

I pray that they will all be one, just as you and I are one—as you are in me, Father, and I am in you. And may they be in us so that the world will believe you sent me. (John 17:21)

God has united you with Christ Jesus. For our benefit God made him to be wisdom itself. Christ made us right with God; he made us pure and holy, and he freed us from sin.
(1 Corinthians 1:30)

You may also hear the word "mantle," which is an assignment, role, or position that can be transferred to another. For example, my parents transferred their mantle or assignment from God to me. This is very similar to the anointing that passed from my parents. The mantle "covers" a person. Scripturally, the story of Elijah and Elisha in 2 Kings, chapter 2, talks about the transference of the mantle from mentor to student.

The anointing (or ministry) you sow into is the anointing you will receive from God. This is a powerful revelation. If you support, assist, help, and pray for a healing ministry like Joan Hunter Ministries, you will receive the same anointing to heal the sick. Of course, you have to recognize, receive, and choose to operate in that anointing. If you choose to ignore it, it will go away.

What Are a Believer's Spiritual Gifts?

But the manifestation of the Spirit is given to each one for the profit of all: for to one is given the word of wisdom through the Spirit, to another the word of knowledge through the same Spirit, to another faith by the same Spirit, to another gifts of healings by the same Spirit, to another the working of miracles, to another prophecy, to another discerning of spirits, to another different kinds of tongues, to another the interpretation of tongues. But one and the same Spirit works all these things, distributing to each one individually as He wills.

(1 Corinthians 12:7–11)

God's Word plainly describes the gifts He gives you. Where He assigns, He also provides. Often, provision is thought of as money or finances, but He also provides the tools and abilities you need to succeed in your assignment. In this case, what He provides the believer are spiritual gifts that the world doesn't understand. He gives you the anointing to walk in and use these special abilities.

SPEAKING IN TONGUES

One of the key signs or manifestation of the baptism of the Holy Spirit is speaking in tongues. By turning over control of your tongue (speech) to God, you give His Spirit permission to speak in a language you do not understand or normally speak. Thus, you are praying (speaking) to God in a language only He can understand.

When someone needs prayer but gives you no details, what do you say? Are you going to use some generic words such as, "Bless them, Lord"? Details are not necessary when you pray in tongues. You can say, "Father, this prayer is for Sue . . . or John . . . or William . . . or Mary." (Fill in the appropriate name, and then pray in tongues.)

For if you have the ability to speak in tongues you will be talking only to God, since people won't be able to understand you. You will be speaking by the power of the Spirit, but it will all be mysterious. (1 Corinthians 14:2)

For if I pray in tongues, my spirit is praying, but I don't understand what I am saying. Well then, what shall I do? I will pray in the spirit, and I will also pray in words I understand. I will sing in the spirit, and I will also sing in words I understand. (1 Corinthians 14:14–15)

Only God will understand when you speak in tongues. You will strengthen yourself personally and often be overcome with His wonderful peace and love. You can also whisper in tongues, sing in tongues, or yell in tongues—whatever you wish. God hears you regardless of the volume.

But you, dear friends, must build each other up in your most holy faith, pray in the power of the Holy Spirit. (Jude 1:20)

INTERPRETATION OF TONGUES

If someone gives a message in tongues (an unknown language) to the body of Christ in a meeting, The Bible instructs that there must be an interpretation of the message so everyone will understand. One person gives the message in tongues and usually another person will give the interpretation (what they feel in their spirit that God is saying to His people). These messages usually encourage the body; however, sometimes God will speak strong words to correct or admonish with love.

Only "approved" people are allowed to give the interpretation (such as a respected church leader). The enemy could cause havoc in a church if anyone off the street was allowed to speak without the permission of the church leadership.

If someone gives a message in tongues in a meeting, the Bible instructs that there must be an interpretation so everyone will understand. One person gives the message in tongues and usually another person will give the interpretation (what they feel in their spirit that God is saying to His people). Only "approved" people are allowed to give the interpretation (such as a respected church leader). The enemy could cause havoc in a church if anyone off the street was allowed to speak without the permission of the church leadership.

WORDS OF WISDOM AND KNOWLEDGE

God may give information to a person who knows nothing about you. If God reveals something about your past, it usually relates to something happening in your life in the present. This is called a word of knowledge because it is divine revelation. Closely related is a word of wisdom which is information about the future and how to use the knowledge you received from God. Only you can confirm the accuracy or validity of the words they speak.

If either of these gifts manifest in a group meeting, one or more people may respond to the message. If the message is truly from God, you will recognize it as a confirmation to a prayer or question in your mind that you haven't even verbalized.

A vision may manifest like a word of wisdom or word of knowledge; however, it can also be something very personal that God shows you about your own life. He may show you a scene of something that may occur in the future to prepare you or prove Who He is. Only He knows your future. Only He can give you your vision or revelation for what is to come. Someone else may "see" you doing something which may seem to be a word of wisdom or knowledge.

I have a "vision" for my ministry. This means I am envisioning what I would like the ministry to develop into in the future. Call it a dream if you want, but I believe it is directly from God. He is showing me what to prepare for in the future. God gives big dreams, so be prepared to do BIG things for Him in your future also.

PROPHECY

Let love be your highest goal! But you should also desire the special abilities the Spirit gives —especially the ability to prophesy. But one who prophesies strengthens others, encourages them, and comforts them. A person who speaks in tongues is strengthened personally, but one who speaks a word of prophecy strengthens the entire church. I wish you could all speak in tongues, but even more I wish you could all prophesy. For prophecy is greater than speaking in tongues, unless someone interprets what you are saying so that the whole church will be strengthened.
(1 Corinthians 14:1, 3–5)

95

Prophecy is for others—to encourage them, to strengthen them, and to give them peace. A prophecy is a message concerning the future. It usually gives direction. A word of wisdom and a prophecy could be very close in meaning; however, a prophecy is usually more involved and longer in length.

You can prophesy to yourself; however, most prophecies are given for another person. (Keep in mind that prophesy is the verb or action, while prophecy is the noun or what is given.) Before you ever act on a prophecy given to you, ask God for guidance. It should confirm something you have been praying about or something God has been telling you from another direction.

Yes, young people get "confirmed" when they join a church in their teens following instruction on the church and basic Christianity. But this type of confirmation is different; it is meant to show something to be true, firm, or valid with several witnesses or tests. For instance, you might receive the same results with several tests of an object. You may check a reservation more than once to confirm it. Many witnesses all give the same account of an event. Pictures can confirm a verbal description as valid.

God wrote in His Word that there should be two or three witnesses before action should be taken on a matter.

But if you are unsuccessful, take one or two others with you and go back again, so that everything you say may be confirmed by two or three witnesses. (Matthew 18:16)

The facts of every case must be established by the testimony of two or three witnesses. (2 Corinthians 13:1)

You have heard me teach things that have been confirmed by many reliable witnesses. Now teach these truths to other

trustworthy people who will be able to pass them on to others.
(2 Timothy 2:2)

You are able to utilize this concept somewhat the same way. You may have been asking God for an answer to a particular situation. You might turn on the TV and someone is teaching on that exact subject. You could open your Bible randomly and read words explaining what you were asking.

When you go to church on Sunday, you might receive a prophecy that has been given to the church or to you individually, and that prophecy will line up with the other information you have heard or read.

The message or answer to your question should be confirmed by three witnesses from different directions. And this confirmation can even occur before you talk to other people about the situation. A prophecy after you have given a detailed explanation to other people may not be words from God, just gossip.

Any prophecy that you receive or hear must be tested against the Word of God, the Bible. You can always discuss it with your mentor as well.

Someone came up to a gentleman one day and said, "God said you were supposed to give me your car." His response was, "Well, I will do it as soon as God tells me to give it to you." This is an example of manipulation, not a word from God.

Do not accept a prophecy, word of wisdom, or word of knowledge from someone with a questionable or unknown character, because the enemy does use people to manipulate actions. Test every word against the Word of God and your spirit. As a new Christian, seek the advice of your mentor. Personal words whether prophecy, wisdom or knowledge from God gives encouragement, instructs, and builds you up. They never manipulate you.

DISCERNMENT

Discernment is another important word you need to understand. Have you ever been in an environment or with a person who makes you very uncomfortable? They might not have outwardly done anything to you or said anything, but you just don't feel comfortable in the situation.

Perhaps, words are spoken that just don't sit right with you. Wiktionary defines discernment as "the ability to make wise judgments."[1] Ask yourself, "Is this situation from God or the enemy?"

When your sensitivity matures, you can recognize if a person is a believer or not. The Jesus in you recognizes the Jesus in the next person. Or the enemy in them recognizes the Jesus in you and responds in a disrespectful manner. You don't understand the hostility because you haven't done anything to the person.

Because the enemy hates the people of God, he works through his unsaved children of disobedience with words of discord and anger. Satan knows the power of Jesus you have inside you, and he wants to distract you.

You may hear the words "spirit of the anti-christ." That simply means someone who is against Christ. And who is the number one entity fighting God and Jesus? Satan, of course. So, the "spirit of the anti-christ" is one of the enemy's demons.

But we belong to God, and those who know God listen to us. If they do not belong to God, they do not listen to us. That is how we know if someone has the Spirit of truth or the spirit of deception. (1 John 4:6)

---

1   Wiktionary, used under the under the Creative Commons Attribution/Share-Alike License, http://en.wiktionary.org/wiki/discernment.

FAITH

Wiktionary defines faith as "A feeling, conviction, or belief that something is true or real, not contingent upon reason or justification."[1] Scripture explains faith as hope in what we cannot see.

> *Faith is the confidence that what we hope for will actually happen; it gives us assurance about things we cannot see.* (Hebrews 11:1)

Before salvation, man lives with a "show me" attitude or a "prove it to me" stance. Once Jesus enters your life, you just know that you know He is real and living inside you. Confidence in God soars to ever increasing heights as you recognize His hand in your life, both past and present. You see with spiritual eyes, His eyes. Read Hebrews 11. It is also called the "Faith Hall of Fame"; it talks about the faith of many great men and women of the Bible.

Faith is very important in a Christian's life. You were saved by faith and live by faith in an invisible God. You believe He will do what He says He will do and live every day by His Word. Because you believe in Him without question, you can accept and use all the gifts available to His children.

HEALING

Yes, healing is a precious gift from God. Even though there have been great men of God who have laid hands on thousands and seen marvelous healings, this gift is not limited to a few. For example, my mother and father, Charles and Frances Hunter, had a worldwide healing ministry. They laid hands on thousands and saw endless

---

1   Wiktionary, used under the under the Creative Commons Attribution/Share-Alike License, http://en.wiktionary.org/wiki/faith.

healings throughout their many years of ministry. They loved what they did, and God honored them with long life and great success in their assignment.

They adopted the saying, "If Charles and Frances can do it, you can do it, too!" Their ministry exploded as they taught believers around the world to do the same thing as they did. They multiplied themselves just as Jesus did through His disciples. My mom and dad knew ministering healing to the world's sick and hurting was too much for them to accomplish. They trained thousands to lay hands on the sick and expect total recovery. I am continuing on in their footsteps with their anointing to teach a new generation to get healed and free and share the word of healing with everyone they meet or touch.

Paul went in and prayed for him, and laying his hands on him, he healed him. (Acts 28:8)

They will lay hands on the sick, and they will recover. (Mark 16:18, NKJV)

Who Himself bore our sins in His own body on the tree, that we, having died to sins, might live for righteousness—by whose stripes you were healed. (1 Peter 2:24, NKJV)

Through the years, some argued with supernatural healing. They claimed it occurred only during Jesus' three years of ministry on the earth. "It isn't for today," they say. But Jesus lives in you, correct? Who does the healing, you or Jesus working through you? So, Jesus still does the healing, doesn't He? He has never changed!

Jesus Christ is the same yesterday, today, and forever. (Hebrews 13:8)

His disciples were sent throughout the countryside to heal the sick and cast out demons just using Jesus' name. At that point, they didn't have Jesus' Spirit living inside of them to give them supernatural power, wisdom, or any gifts or fruit of the Spirit. They didn't receive the Holy Spirit's baptism until the day of Pentecost, fifty days after Jesus ascended into heaven. Of course, they used all those gifts from then on until their death.

How Can We Receive Healing from Past Hurts?

Life doesn't exist without good and bad things happening. After all, how would you appreciate the good things if nothing negative ever happened to you? Many things can simply be shaken off and forgotten; however, some events open the door for long-lasting effects on your life. If not handled appropriately, they will affect your life from that time on.

Some people suffer from life-long problems. One simple prayer frees them from the bondage and pain. Their facial expression changes, their posture changes, and they have a new life from that day onward. Years seem to drop off their total appearance after ministry.

Are you willing and ready to be healed from the inside out? Some seem to enjoy being sick because of the attention they receive, the excuse not to do more for the kingdom, or because of the handicap parking sticker in their car window. Please, don't fall into that trap of the enemy.

Part of the enemy's arsenal is negative spirits of depression, fear, pain, anger, hate, resentment, manipulation, stress, trauma, abuse, shame, and guilt. There are many more, but these are the most common that we deal with on a regular basis. Generational curses are passed through the bloodline from our ancestors' sins. Soul ties, unholy covenants, and word curses have to be revoked.

Some churches call this process "Freedom Ministry" because you are set free from all the negative influences. Some call it deliverance because you are literally being delivered or loosened from these spirits or demons of the enemy who only want to destroy you.

You may also hear the term "emotional healing." Abusive relationships, whether they are child, adult, or spousal abuse, leave deep scars that can prevent or destroy future relationships. Only the unconditional love of the Father can supernaturally heal many of these unseen, hidden, and painful memories and emotions, because they can pursue the abused person for a lifetime.

The enemy only knows how to lie, kill, and destroy. Even Christians are plagued with the enemy's lies that tempt a believer to entertain negative thoughts and behavior. If you aren't wearing your armor or staying connected to God, the Source of all Light and Life, you will be susceptible to the enemy's lies, which will lead to destruction.

Does God Speak to Us in Our Dreams?

Some people dream, and some don't. Some of these dreams are messages from God. Most aren't. Remembering your dream is often the challenge.

Interpretation of these dreams is a specialty in itself. There are a few people in the body of Christ who have been blessed with the capability of interpreting dreams; however, just like visions and Words of Knowledge or Wisdom, you must weigh the words carefully.

Dreams should be a confirmation of other similar messages from God, not just the result of indigestion from last night's dinner.

The most famous dreamer in the Bible was Joseph. Unfortunately, or perhaps due to his youth, he misinterpreted the meaning of his dreams and got himself into serious trouble. When mature, his dream finally came to pass and his gift promoted him to Pharaoh's second in command. Knowing when to act is very important with dream interpretation.

> No, what you see was predicted long ago by the prophet Joel: "In the last days," God says, "I will pour out my Spirit upon all people. Your sons and daughters will prophesy. Your young men will see visions, and your old men will dream dreams. In those days I will pour out my Spirit even on my servants—men and women alike—and they will prophesy."
> (Acts 2:16–18)

Who Are Spiritual Gifts For?

The gifts of the Spirit are tools you need and use when ministering to others. Yes, they are of benefit to you as a believer; however, they are for others. They are considered "signs and wonders" to draw the unbeliever to Christ.

> They were convinced by the power of miraculous signs and wonders and by the power of God's Spirit. (Romans 15:19)

> But the apostles stayed there a long time, preaching boldly about the grace of the Lord. And the Lord proved their message was true by giving them power to do miraculous signs and wonders. (Acts 14:3)

> When I was with you, I certainly gave you proof that I am an apostle. For I patiently did many signs and wonders and miracles among you. (2 Corinthians 12:12)

> And God confirmed the message by giving signs and wonders and various miracles and gifts of the Holy Spirit whenever he chose. (Hebrews 2:4)

For God is not the author of confusion but of peace, as in all the churches of the saints. (1 Corinthians 14:33, NKJV)

SECTION FIVE

THE SUPERNATURAL

What Is The Supernatural?

The word supernatural means something that is beyond the natural; it is something that is unexplainable with usual logic or laws of physics or science. It may be described as a phenomenon or something extraordinary or unbelievable, or even something that exists above and beyond nature as we know it.

The supernatural that comes from God is beautiful, good, wonderful, and a blessing. And man is a supernatural being. Man is an eternal spirit who lives in an earthly body and has a soul made up of a will, mind, and emotions. The body ages, wears out, and dies along with the soul. But the spirit is eternal, and you have to choose where you will spend eternity: with the God of light and love or with the enemy in darkness and hell.

What Is the Difference Between Light and Darkness?

Anything to do with God, Jesus, or the Holy Spirit is often described as "light." Pictures of heaven show rays of beautiful light, which symbolize openness, honesty, truth, and goodness. Angels from God are always surrounded by light, versus the "dark" or hidden things of the enemy. Even though Satan is described in Scripture as light, he is the epitome of darkness and evil and is often symbolized by scary objects of the night such as snakes, owls, frogs, toads, and demons. He may appear as something beautiful because he often imitates God; however, he is not the Creator.

God is light, and there is no darkness in him at all. So we are lying if we say we have fellowship with God but go on living in spiritual darkness; we are not practicing the truth. But if we are living in the light, as God is in the light, then we have fellowship with each other, and the blood of Jesus, his Son, cleanses us from all sin. (1 John 1:5–7)

God's spotlight will reveal truth as well as evil. Don't think evil will remain hidden. God knows. Once you are saved and walking in His light, don't even consider falling back to your old life. Turn your back and walk away from temptation. Stay in His light!

Don't be fooled by those who try to excuse these sins, for the anger of God will fall on all who disobey him. Don't participate in the things these people do. For once you were full of darkness, but now you have light from the Lord. So live as people of light! For this light within you produces only what is good and right and true. Carefully determine what pleases the Lord. Take no part in the worthless deeds of evil and darkness; instead, expose them. It is shameful even to talk about the things that ungodly people do in secret. But their evil intentions will be exposed when the light shines on them, for the light makes everything visible. This is why it is said, "Awake, O sleeper, rise up from the dead, and Christ will give you light." (Ephesians 5:6–14)

What Are Angels?

Archangels, seraphim, and cherubim are a few of the categories of angels within God's organization in heaven. There are ministering angels, those who bring messages to the earth, and warriors who fight for us. And there are likely many more that we will not know of until we reach heaven. It is hypothesized that they travel at a much higher speed than we do; thus, they are invisible to us mortals on the earth.

Angelic visitations are documented from the Old Testament through the modern day. Because God is all-powerful, He can send His angels wherever He chooses. If a human doesn't respond to instructions in certain situations, He may have to send an angel.

Some humans seem to be angels as they appear out of nowhere and do something or give you something at just the right moment.

> *In the same way, there is joy in the presence of God's angels when even one sinner repents.* (Luke 15:9–10)

Scripture tells us they protect, they rejoice, they proclaim, and they deliver people and messages. God created angels to carry out His assignments in heaven and on the earth. They have been seen in meetings. For example, my parents had two giant warrior angels who traveled with them for years. I am sure these same angels carried Mom and Dad home when God called them also.

> *For the Scriptures say, "He will order his angels to protect and guard you."* (Luke 4:10)

> *In my desperation I prayed, and the Lord listened; he saved me from all my troubles. For the angel of the Lord is a guard; he surrounds and defends all who fear him.* (Psalm 34:6–7)

> *Therefore, angels are only servants—spirits sent to care for people who will inherit salvation.* (Hebrews 1:14)

According to the book of Hebrews, everyone who is or will be saved has an angel who looks out for their welfare. They are God's servants. Man doesn't order angels around; however, you can certainly ask God to give them special assignments. At the same time, don't expect their divine intervention or assistance unless you are walking in obedience to God's Word. Like any of God's blessings, you receive them when you are under His umbrella of protection and serving Him.

What Are the Blessings of God?

Put on His blessings. His Word changes and renews your mind daily to be more and more like Christ. What do I mean by "put on"? Receive His blessings. He gave you life. He gives you the gift of every breath. He is a generous Father to His children. Choose to walk in His blessings. Recognize all His blessings that surround you daily. And thank Him for each and every one of them.

> *I said to the Lord, "You are my Master! Every good thing I have comes from you."* (Psalm 16:2)

Blessings of the world are temporary. Blessings from God are eternal and will go on forever. Deuteronomy 28 has a long list of His blessings as a reward for obedience. In short, every positive thing we receive is from God, and these are His blessings.

> *Today I have given you the choice between life and death, between blessings and curses. Now I call on heaven and earth to witness the choice you make. Oh, that you would choose life, so that you and your descendants might live!* (Deuteronomy 30:19)

> *All praise to God, the Father of our Lord Jesus Christ, who has blessed us with every spiritual blessing in the heavenly realms because we are united with Christ.* (Ephesians 1:3)

> *All who are victorious will inherit all these blessings, and I will be their God, and they will be my children.* (Revelation 21:7)

Does God Have an Assignment for Me?

Occasionally, you will hear a Christian say, "God called me when I was a child." Now, whether that person followed God's path to their ultimate assignment is part of their individual testimony. Some do, and some don't. The prayers of your parents or grandparents will follow you wherever you go and whatever you do. God will send His people and/or angels to guide you back to Him.

You do have a God-ordained assignment. Talk to Him. A mentor or leader may see something in you that could reveal what God has planned, but you have to accept it and develop it. Recognize His assignment and eliminate other distractions that come your way. Be determined to focus on God's plan for you. Seek His voice. Confirm His message to you.

Each of you should continue to live in whatever situation the Lord has placed you, and remain as you were when God first called you. This is my rule for all the churches. Yes, each of you should remain as you were when God called you.
(1 Corinthians 7:17, 20)

God is not telling you to stay in your present job forever. Some people get saved, quit their job, and jump into ministry without preparation. God may be calling you into fulltime ministry, but His timing is important. You must be ready, or the enemy will crush you like a bug. You wouldn't squash a child's dream to become a doctor, but you wouldn't send a child to medical school the first time they mention their dream either. Training, growth, maturity, wisdom, and timing are all vital to success.

God may have you in a particular job to touch a particular person. Stay where you are until God clearly directs you to leave. He knows you need an income to eat and live on. Don't rush. Let God lead you. Don't run ahead of Him, or you will be outside of His will and protection. He opens doors. He closes doors. He will give you favor as long as you are obedient.

When His plan is clear, it becomes your vision. From then on, your plans of life need to line up with the vision He has given you. You will find passages in Scripture to support that vision. From that revelation, your mission statement will be formulated. A mission statement clearly outlines your goals of life and ministry: both your mission and your assignment.

SECTION SIX

SPIRITUAL WARFARE

What Is Spiritual Warfare?

Before you invited Jesus into your heart, you were living in the kingdom of darkness. Remember, darkness indicates the enemy, the devil or Satan. He was the serpent who enticed Eve to sin way back in the book of Genesis. Through Adam and Eve, sin entered the earth and has been present since that day.

Man is actually surrounded with the supernatural realm of God. You can't see the wind; however, you know it is real because you can see its effects and feel it. You can't see God, but you can see what He does and feel His presence.

There is a battle going on continuously. God, Jesus, the Holy Spirit, His angels, and believers are on one side. Satan, his demonic angels, and his followers (those who don't believe in or do not have Jesus living within them) are on the other side. You cannot see Satan; however, you can see what he does.

How Can You Distinguish an Angel of Light?

> *These people are false apostles. They are deceitful workers who disguise themselves as apostles of Christ. But I am not surprised! Even Satan disguises himself as an angel of light. So it is no wonder that his servants also disguise themselves as servants of righteousness. In the end they will get the punishment their wicked deeds deserve.* (2 Corinthians 11:13–15).

When you are saved and have Jesus' Spirit within you, your eyes are opened to the spirit world. No, you are not going to see ghosts floating around you; however, you will recognize the effects of the enemy versus those of God, and you will recognize His hand working around you and for you. You will know His voice.

115

To open their eyes, so they may turn from darkness to light and from the power of Satan to God. Then they will receive forgiveness for their sins and be given a place among God's people, who are set apart by faith in me. (Acts 26:18)

How do you know what is of God and what is not? In every situation, ask the question, "What Would Jesus Do?" If something doesn't line up with the Word of God, it is definitely not of God.

And now, dear brothers and sisters, one final thing. Fix your thoughts on what is true, and honorable, and right, and pure, and lovely, and admirable. Think about things that are excellent and worthy of praise. Keep putting into practice all you learned and received from me—everything you heard from me and saw me doing. Then the God of peace will be with you. (Philippians 4: 8–9)

Every good and perfect gift comes from God. If you are in a situation that is not following or agreeing with the Ten Commandments or other instructions within the Bible, you are facing a temptation sent by the enemy. God doesn't tempt you.

God has given man free choice. You can choose to follow the ruler of darkness, Satan, or the ruler of the universe, God. God doesn't tempt man; however, He won't step into your situation immediately to remove all obstacles or mountains from your path. He wants to see your reaction to a challenge. What choice will you make?

No one can serve two masters. For you will hate one and love the other; you will be devoted to one and despise the other. You cannot serve both God and money. (Matthew 6:24)

Are you going to look to the world for answers? The world is controlled by the enemy. Are you going to look to God's Word and listen for His voice for the best way for you to handle the challenge? Are you going to claim His protection and stand on His promises? Keep in mind that God wants only the best for His children. He wants you to prosper. (See Jeremiah 29:11.)

What does Satan want you to do? He wants you to follow him into hell. He is fighting to destroy you and your relationship with the Father. When he wanted to rule heaven, his rebellious behavior sent him crashing to the earth. God kicked Satan out of His presence, and he will do anything to rob you of your inheritance and your position with God.

One-third of heaven's angels fell with him. They are now called demonic angels. They were once God's angels in heaven, but they placed their allegiance and trust in the wrong voice. Satan is the father of lies, hate, anger, pain, and murder, all the ugly things leading to destruction and hell.

> *"Yes," he told them, "I saw Satan fall from heaven like lightning! Look, I have given you authority over all the power of the enemy, and you can walk among snakes and scorpions and crush them. Nothing will injure you. But don't rejoice because evil spirits obey you; rejoice because your names are registered in heaven."* (Luke 10:18–19)

> *For you are the children of your father the devil, and you love to do the evil things he does. He was a murderer from the beginning. He has always hated the truth, because there is no truth in him. When he lies, it is consistent with his character; for he is a liar and the father of lies.* (John 8:44)

Anything bad or ugly comes from the enemy. It doesn't come from your spouse or in-laws, even if the words may come from their mouths.

What Is the Armor of God?

Put on the whole armor of God, that you may be able to stand against the wiles of the devil. For we do not wrestle against flesh and blood, but against principalities, against powers, against the rulers of the darkness of this age, against spiritual hosts of wickedness in the heavenly places. Therefore, put on every piece of God's armor so you will be able to resist the enemy in the time of evil. Then after the battle you will still be standing firm. Stand your ground, putting on the belt of truth and the body armor of God's righteousness. For shoes, put on the peace that comes from the Good News so that you will be fully prepared. In addition to all of these, hold up the shield of faith to stop the fiery arrows of the devil. Put on salvation as your helmet, and take the sword of the Spirit, which is the word of God. Pray in the Spirit at all times and on every occasion. Stay alert and be persistent in your prayers for all believers everywhere. (Ephesians 6:11–18)

Putting on the armor of God is not difficult. Start at the top of your head and work your way down saying, "Father, I put on the helmet of salvation and the breastplate of righteousness. I put on the belt of truth and shoes of peace. I have the shield of faith in one hand and the sword of the Spirit (the Word of God) in the other. I will pray in the Spirit and have Your praise on my lips. I'm ready to go!"

God has outlined the battle plan and given you His suggested uniform and weapons. It is your choice to be obedient and wear your armor every day. The enemy doesn't tell you which way he is coming from or what his latest subtle tactic will be.

Satan is crafty, sly, deceptive, and totally unable to create anything new. He only copies what he has seen before, which means he imitates God in many ways.

When you are tempted by Satan to do something questionable, don't avoid the mountain. Confront the challenge, speak His Word, and remove the obstacle. This exercise develops character and helps you to grow. Every promotion is made through a battleground. God wants you to grow and advance towards the best you can be. The enemy is trying to destroy you and separate you from your Father.

> *The temptations in your life are no different from what others experience. And God is faithful. He will not allow the temptation to be more than you can stand. When you are tempted, he will show you a way out so that you can endure.* (1 Corinthians 10:13)

> *But you, Timothy, are a man of God; so run from all these evil things. Pursue righteousness and a godly life, along with faith, love, perseverance, and gentleness.* (1 Timothy 6:12)

You aren't fighting with guns and knives; you are fighting with God's Word and faith in Him. Doing things God's way brings blessings. Failure to follow God's instructions will result in losing His protection and blessings. Do you think you know better than God? Do you have a better answer? You may be operating in pride, which results in decreased blessings and rebellion. Pride is one of Satan's lies.

Operating outside of God's Word will bring ultimate failure. Satan's number one goal is to separate you from God and His Word. That's his job. Even Satan has a purpose. How can man choose if there aren't two paths to follow? Choose life, or choose death. There isn't a middle ground. Either you are serving God or Satan. You can't stay neutral.

Your discernment must differentiate between God's voice and a god's voice. You must know who you are listening to. Yes, there are "gods" of this world. What does man worship? Money, objects, toys, cars, sports, mansions, and prestige are but a few of the things that captivate the heart, mind, and soul of many.

But let us who live in the light be clearheaded, protected by the armor of faith and love, and wearing as our helmet the confidence of our salvation. (1 Thessalonians 5:8)

Education often shuts off the communication between God and His children. Logic, science, philosophy, and the world's wisdom believe man can do things better than God. Their fancy words and convincing logic blurs focus and faith in Almighty God.

Who gave them their intelligence? Who blessed them with educational opportunities? Who led the colonists from a repressed society to the shores of the United States where freedom allowed an explosion of life and technology?

Today's worldview gives man credit where God is the ultimate Instigator and Creator of our current environment. So, know who you are listening to. The Bible is a ruler. Measure everything against the Bible. Does it agree with God's Word? Or is it taking you another direction?

Don't do anything without knowing God's will for your situation. As you learn more about His Word, living in freedom within His guidelines is easier and easier every day. Doing things based on your own knowledge and pride is a form of witchcraft.

When you have God's mark of salvation and your eyes are open to the truth, Satan does get upset. He had great plans of destruction for you, and you are no longer cooperating with him. God has important plans for your life (see Jeremiah 29:11). Does the enemy cower away in defeat? No; rather, he may attack from the opposite direction, using anything to distract you. The devil will talk about your past failures and negative behavior. God talks about your future success and His vision for your life. You can't focus in both directions at the same time. How you relate to your past determines your reaction to your future. Ignore distractions. Focus on God.

Your family may think you are crazy for getting saved. People at work may make fun of you. The kids may even fight all the way to church. Strange evil thoughts run through your head especially when you are trying to concentrate on reading the Bible or listen to the pastor's message in church. You haven't had a drink or a cigarette in years; however, suddenly the craving comes over you like a flood. What is happening? The enemy is fighting back. He knows God has something good coming your way. If he can derail you and cause you to leave God's protection, your blessings won't reach you, or they will be delayed.

Satan cannot make you do anything. There is a saying, "The devil made me do it!" But it is a lie straight from the pit of hell! You are responsible for your actions. You choose to follow the bad thoughts that pop into your head, or you choose to rebuke them with the Word of God.

God tells us to pray without ceasing. Do you wonder why? Because prayer keeps the enemy away. He can't stand hearing the name of Jesus. He runs when voices are raised in praise and worship towards heaven.

Through the praise of children and infants you have established a stronghold against your enemies, to silence the foe and the avenger. (Psalm 8:2, NIV)

What Weapons Does the Devil Use Against Me?

The devil can't read your mind, but he does hear your voice. You tell somebody your fears and concerns, and he will use that information against you. He can drop things into your mind that magnify his characteristics such as fear, frustration, discouragement, depression, hate, anger, and lies: "You aren't good enough! God doesn't want you! You are worthless! Tell that person what you really think about them! They hurt you! Kill him! You'll never get healed! You might as well die!"

What Weapons Do I Have?

Spiritually, put on the armor of God every day. Speak it aloud as you visualize yourself putting on each piece. With His praise on your lips, start your day!

Ask yourself where those negative thoughts came from, and what is the purpose or intention of those thoughts. And ask yourself what will be the result if you act on those things: will they cause confusion or peace, and are they from God or the enemy?

Your mouth is a weapon. Your words are the edge of the sword! The Word of God is the ammunition! Where do you win a battle? Do you wait to prepare in the field facing the enemy? No, you prepare before you hit the arena.

What sports team would face an opponent without preparation or practice? None. What military unit would fight without a plan or strategy or without knowing how to handle their weapons of destruction? None.

You must prepare for the battle because it will come. Problems are part of life. Challenges either develop your maturity and help you reach your next level, or they neutralize you. Trouble doesn't destroy you; however, your response to your challenge may. It is your choice to believe God or the enemy. (God wins every time!)

When you recognize ideas or thoughts are not from God, fight back! Speak the Word of God. Put on praise and worship music. Pray in tongues.

> *For though we walk in the flesh, we do not war according to the flesh. For the weapons of our warfare are not carnal but mighty in God for pulling down strongholds, casting down arguments and every high thing that exalts itself against the knowledge of God, bringing every thought into captivity to the obedience of Christ.* (2 Corinthians 10:3–5, NKJV)

What does this verse mean? You can't fight spiritual battles using any weapon from the natural world. You must use the weapons God has given to you. His Word is the greatest tool you have in your arsenal. The Bible tells you what to do.

Drive out the thoughts not of God. Read the Bible out loud so you will be seeing it, saying it, and hearing it at the same time. Talk to yourself in the mirror. Pray.

Declare these words out loud, "I am the righteousness of God in Christ. God is my Father. Jesus is my Lord. Holy Spirit, You are my Counselor and Comforter. I walk and talk in Your wisdom and understanding. My faith is in You. I claim Your protection according to Malachi 3:10."

Remember, just the name of Jesus makes the enemy run the other direction. Jesus has authority over the devil. Jesus gave us His authority to tread on scorpions and snakes, meaning the devil and his demons. Use your authority! Stomp! If you can't think of anything else, just say "Jesus" over and over.

Just as physical battles cause stress, drain energy, and can result in injury, spiritual battles can do the same. Each person has to learn to fight their own battles and stand up to the enemy. You can explain, instruct, and counsel. Most importantly, you can pray. Don't accept false responsibility for someone else's battle.

Be careful which fight you choose to join. Don't fight someone else's battle, or you will invite trouble upon yourself that you weren't designed to handle. Stay in your own arena. Each person has their own things to deal with. Listen to God. Yes, you can pray with and for someone. You can encourage them in their situation. But please, learn to pick your battles.

> *For every child of God defeats this evil world, and we achieve this victory through our faith.* (1 John 5:4)

What Should My Priorities Be?

As in any activity of life, you must choose your priorities. What is the most important thing to do first? What can wait until later? Run all activities through the priority grid. Will this activity affect my relationship with God or man? Will the influence be negative or positive? Keep your priorities straight.

The most important priority in the life of a Christian is God. He is number one forever. (Check the Ten Commandments.) Following God, your priorities are your spouse, family, church, work, etc. If you get your priorities out of order, your life will not flow well. Conflict will enter.

There is a difference between working for God and with God. If your employment is in a ministry, differentiating between these two positions can be difficult. You must go to God Himself first for instruction. Minister or pay attention to your family's needs, then your church and work. God will never direct you to spend so much time and energy "working" for a church or ministry that you neglect your family.

You must put on Christ every day. You must determine to walk like Christ, talk like Christ, and react to challenges like He did. Christ quoted the Word back to Satan. He always spoke peace and love.

How Should I Use the Word of God?

The Word of God is the most effective weapon you have in your arsenal to fight the enemy. He doesn't like to hear the Word of God. Even Jesus used the Word of God to fight the enemy in the desert when He was tempted. If this weapon was effective for the Son of God to use, you can use it just as well. (Read about Jesus being tempted in the desert in Matthew 4:1–11.):

> *But the Lord is faithful; he will strengthen you and guard you from the evil one.* (2 Thessalonians 3:3)

> *Fight the good fight for the true faith. Hold tightly to the eternal life to which God has called you, which you have confessed so well before many witnesses.* (2 Timothy 6:12)

> *But he gives us even more grace to stand against such evil desires. As the Scriptures say, "God opposes the proud but favors the humble." So humble yourselves before God. Resist the devil, and he will flee from you.* (James 4:6–7)

How Should I Use Jesus' Name?

> *But these are written so that you may continue to believe that Jesus is the Messiah, the Son of God, and that by believing in him you will have life by the power of his name.* (John 20:31)

The name of Jesus is powerful. He sits at the right hand of the Ruler of the universe. Jesus has all authority, second only to God. God gave authority to Adam in the book of Genesis. But Adam gave it away. In order for it to return to man, God had to come to the earth in the form of His Son. Jesus gave His chosen, us, authority to rule the earth. So what have you done lately to clean things up? People on the earth, even the Christians sitting in the church pews, have no idea what authority they have within their reach.

One day Jesus called together his twelve disciples and gave them power and authority to cast out all demons and to heal all diseases. (Luke 9:1)

The disciples saw Jesus do many other miraculous signs in addition to the ones recorded in this book. But these are written so that you may continue to believe that Jesus is the Messiah, the Son of God, and that by believing in him you will have life by the power of his name. (John 20:30–31)

Through faith in the name of Jesus, this man was healed— and you know how crippled he was before. Faith in Jesus' name has healed him before your very eyes. (Acts 3:16)

And whatever you ask in My name, that I will do, that the Father may be glorified in the Son. (John 14:13)

And these signs will follow those who believe: In My name they will cast out demons; they will speak with new tongues. (Mark 16:17)

You did not choose Me, but I chose you and appointed you that you should go and bear fruit, and that your fruit should remain, that whatever you ask the Father in My name He may give you. (John 15:16)

Countless testimonies through the years share a common thread: "I was in trouble. All I could think of was to call out the name of Jesus. Suddenly, everything was fine!" The accident was averted. The attacker ran the other direction. Suddenly, help appeared.

Use this powerful weapon. Call on His name: JESUS!

Is There Power in Jesus' Blood?

The precious blood of Jesus is powerful. One drop of His blood changed the world. It still changes things today.

In the Old Testament, the blood of an animal sacrifice was used for forgiveness of sins. As the spotless, perfect sacrifice for mankind for eternity, Jesus' blood was drained from His body at Calvary as He hung on that cross.

His blood covers those who believe in Him. God sees each of us through Jesus' blood sacrifice, which reconciles us back to His presence without sin or blemish.

A powerful weapon to use when you pray is to plead the blood of Jesus over your home, your loved ones, and your property. You are asking for a spiritual shield of protection around what is precious to you. Another way of saying the same thing is to cover someone or something with the blood of Jesus. Without His shed blood, you would not have a chance of ever reaching heaven.

> *So Jesus said again, "I tell you the truth, unless you eat the flesh of the Son of Man and drink his blood, you cannot have eternal life within you." (John 6:53)*

> *But now you have been united with Christ Jesus. Once you were far away from God, but now you have been brought near to him through the blood of Christ. (Ephesians 2:13)*

And so, dear brothers and sisters, we can boldly enter heaven's Most Holy Place because of the blood of Jesus. (Hebrews 10:19)

You have come to Jesus, the one who mediates the new covenant between God and people, and to the sprinkled blood, which speaks of forgiveness instead of crying out for vengeance like the blood of Abel. (Hebrews 12:24)

So also Jesus suffered and died outside the city gates to make his people holy by means of his own blood. (Hebrews, 13:12)

Now may the God of peace — who brought up from the dead our Lord Jesus, the great Shepherd of the sheep, and ratified an eternal covenant with his blood. (Hebrews 13:20)

God the Father knew you and chose you long ago, and his Spirit has made you holy. As a result, you have obeyed him and have been cleansed by the blood of Jesus Christ. May God give you more and more grace and peace. (1 Peter 1:2)

But if we are living in the light, as God is in the light, then we have fellowship with each other, and the blood of Jesus, his Son, cleanses us from all sin. (1 John 1:7)

What Is Communion?

Communion is the most solemn of the sacraments of the church. It reminds every Christian of the ultimate sacrifice of the Lord Jesus Christ when He willingly laid down His life for the salvation of mankind. It is a very serious experience for the believer. Jesus took your punishment for your sins. He took your place on the cross.

This commemorates the Last Supper Jesus shared with His apostles before His crucifixion. As Jesus shared the bread and wine, He gave them final instructions. The wine represented His blood, and the bread represented His body. They did not understand the significance of His words until many days later.

> *As they were eating, Jesus took some bread and blessed it. Then he broke it in pieces and gave it to the disciples, saying, "Take this and eat it, for this is my body." And he took a cup of wine and gave thanks to God for it. He gave it to them and said, "Each of you drink from it, for this is my blood, which confirms the covenant between God and his people. It is poured out as a sacrifice to forgive the sins of many."*
> (Matthew 26:26–28)

Before you take Communion, you must repent for anything you have done contrary to His Word. If you have a problem with another person, you are to take care of that before coming to the Communion table. Each time you participate in Communion with a pure heart, you are becoming more and more like Christ with His DNA.

> *But if we confess our sins to him, he is faithful and just to forgive us our sins and to cleanse us from all wickedness.*
> (1 John 1:9)

The word *Communion* means something is communicated or shared with intimacy and spiritual closeness. During this sacrament, God sees you through the blood of Jesus. His blood cleanses you from sin. Christians can never forget what Jesus did on Calvary and how important His sacrifice was for each one. Instructions are very plain. You are to remember.

You are reasonable people. Decide for yourselves if what I am saying is true. When we bless the cup at the Lord's Table, aren't we sharing in the blood of Christ? And when we break the bread, aren't we sharing in the body of Christ? And though we are many, we all eat from one loaf of bread, showing that we are one body. (1 Corinthians 10:15–17)

For I pass on to you what I received from the Lord himself. On the night when he was betrayed, the Lord Jesus took some bread and gave thanks to God for it. Then he broke it in pieces and said, "This is my body, which is given for you. Do this to remember me." In the same way, he took the cup of wine after supper, saying, "This cup is the new covenant between God and his people—an agreement confirmed with my blood. Do this to remember me as often as you drink it." For every time you eat this bread and drink this cup, you are announcing the Lord's death until he comes again. (1 Corinthians 11:23–26)

What Is Deliverance?

Deliverance basically means to rescue from captivity or domination. It does go a step further in the Christian world. Specifically, a person is set free from the effects or work of the God's archenemy, the devil.

All good things come from the Father. The bad comes from the enemy. Some of these are effects of sin that carry through the generations. Certain others are the result of demonic spirits entering through life experiences in order to separate you from God.

Everyone has something hanging over his or her life that needs to be taken care of. Through a short interview, things can be identified and disposed of through ministry.

Common spirits are trauma, stress, and fear. Is trauma, stress, or fear from God? No. If they are not from God, the only other source is the enemy. Trauma and stress can cause numerous illnesses. Fear breeds depression, anger, low self-esteem, jealousy, hate, frustration, withdrawal, and aggression. Get rid of them.

If a person is demon possessed, they have allowed the devil to completely take over their life. Their words, their demeanor, their actions, and their personality all portray the enemy. They may seem to have a split personality with normal behavior part of the time.

A Christian cannot be demon possessed. If the Holy Spirit lives within you, the enemy can't. However, the enemy can feed you his lies and "oppress" you. With your God-given discernment, recognize the enemy's lies and activities, and choose to concentrate on God's Word instead.

Dear friends, do not believe everyone who claims to speak by the Spirit. You must test them to see if the spirit they have comes from God. For there are many false prophets in the world. This is how we know if they have the Spirit of God If a person claiming to be a prophet acknowledges that Jesus Christ came in a real body, that person has the Spirit of God. But if someone claims to be a prophet and does not acknowledge the truth about Jesus, that person is not from God. Such a person has the spirit of the Antichrist, which you heard is coming into the world and indeed is already here. (1 John 4:1–3)

So I want you to know that no one speaking by the Spirit of God will curse Jesus, and no one can say Jesus is Lord, except by the Holy Spirit. (1 Corinthians 12:3)

Be a good listener. Use your discernment. Listen to the Holy Spirit. You will not hear a Christian taking the Lord's name in vain or cursing Jesus' name.

What Is Fasting?

Fasting usually brings up visions of refusing food while watching others enjoy delicious delicacies. But it is so much more than that. It is not a physical restriction at all; it is a spiritual experience.

Fasting shouldn't be broadcast to the world. It is a very personal experience between you and God. Fasting doesn't change God or His answer to any situation or prayer. Fasting gives you an opportunity to focus strictly on God. Instead of eating, spend that time talking to God or meditating on His Word. Self-control changes your heart and focuses your mind on God, Who is more important than your physical needs.

There are many things you can fast. Listen to God's voice. Follow His instructions. Maybe He does want you to give up food for a day. Do it privately and quietly. You could fast meat, bread, or desserts.

Perhaps you are spending too much time watching TV when He wants your attention. Don't neglect your time with Him. He wants to communicate with you. Maybe sports consume your time. Is the big game more important than God? Tape the game and watch it later.

Sometimes, you may just need to cut out the entire world. No TV, no radio, no telephone, no texting or e-mail, and no people. God wants to talk to you. He is not in competition with all the technological advances and toys you use during your day. He will patiently wait until the quiet allows you to hear His still small voice.

Pray about fasting. Does God want you to do it? What does He want you to fast? What is the purpose? What is your goal? Don't just jump into it. You won't accomplish anything. Do it God's way and miracles can happen.

What Is Worship?

Worship is actually one of your weapons in your supernatural arsenal to fight the enemy. You may hear the phrase "praise and worship" related to church services and meetings. There is a big difference between the two. You "praise" someone for what they have done. And yes, we do have much to praise God for. The song may be sung fast or slow, but it will tell the story of what happened and how God helped us through a situation. Many great songs through the years are in this category. The songs enthuse, proclaim, encourage, and motivate.

> *Praise the Lord, for the Lord is good; celebrate his lovely name with music.* (Psalm 135:3)

> *Let them praise the Lord for his great love and for the wonderful things he has done for them.* (Psalm 107:31)

Some churches sing two fast songs and three slow songs and stop. If Spirit-led, the praise and worship may go on for an extended period of time. Why? Because the praise rebukes the enemy. He leaves. Hopefully, it drives out the cares of the day and the problems at home or work and refocuses everyone's mind on God. This paves the way into His presence.

True worship takes you a step higher and closer to God's throne room. Since heaven will be filled with pure worship of Him, you need to get used to it while still earthbound. When you worship Him, you do it because of Who He is. Worship brings you closer to Him. It is almost a tangible presence you can reach out and touch.

You can feel Him surrounding you. Nothing else matters as you bask in His love.

A particular worship song may bring you to your knees, but you don't remember kneeling. People get healed in His presence during intense worship. Physical, mental, and emotional changes happen. It is an experience no one can forget. It prepares hearts for the message God wants to bring through the speaker chosen for the gathering. You may cry for no obvious reason, or you may laugh.

During this glorious experience, you may hear people singing in tongues. The sound is more like angels singing in perfect harmony. This, too, brings a stronger presence of God into the room. You don't want it to ever end.

As your personal weapon, keep His praise and worship playing in your home and in your car as you move about. You won't complain and bicker when God's music is playing. Many Christians have His music playing in their home 24/7. You may not be able to hear it from all corners of the house; however, just walking into the home, you know the atmosphere is something very special. You don't want to leave.

To keep yourself focused on God's will for your life and avoid temptation, use His music. Keep your mind on Him. There are many simple songs that are easy to remember. Many are based totally on Scripture, so you are singing His Word. Learn one, then two, and then three songs. When a crisis arises, sing. When faced with a temptation, sing.

A very simple song was popular many years ago. It started out with "God is so good" and went on: "I love you so," "I'll praise Your Name," and "Alleluia." When you worship, you are singing a beautiful love song to your Father and, Jesus, His Son. Your sacrifice of praise in the midst of adversity creates a sweet smelling aroma, which reaches His throne room.

*Therefore, let us offer through Jesus a continual sacrifice of
praise to God, proclaiming our allegiance to his name. And
don't forget to do good and to share with those in need. These
are the sacrifices that please God.* (Hebrews 13:15–16)

Reading that passage may bring up a question. What is a sacrifice of praise? Remember, praise is part of your arsenal. When you are hurting, crying, aching, or grieving, confusion often follows. Who is the author of confusion? Not God. The enemy is attempting to distract and separate you from God. It may not make sense to the world, but praise becomes your weapon. Your heart doesn't feel like any type of praise or worship; however, if you make the choice to open your mouth, the first few words you speak will draw you back into His protection and peace. Your view of the situation changes and confusion flees.

You can understand why music, praise, and worship are very important during church services. It is also very important within your own environment. Hallelujah, Allelujah, and Alleluia all refer to a song or music giving God praise. According to Scripture, you can express your emotions in many ways in church. Before showing too much exuberance during a meeting, however, you should check the group's philosophy. Some do not accept raising your hands, free dancing, flag waving, or clapping during a service. Many speakers appreciate hearing an "Amen!" when you heartily agree with what they are saying; however, others feel they are being rudely interrupted.

*Then I will praise you with music on the harp, because you
are faithful to your promises, O my God. I will sing praises
to you with a lyre, O Holy One of Israel. I will shout for joy
and sing your praises, for you have ransomed me.* (Psalm 71:
22–23)

Instruments and worship bands are more commonplace today and are scriptural. The regal sound of pipe organs was not available in biblical times. They used small homemade instruments such as tambourines, the lyre, rams' horns, and drums. Singing and clapping were obviously the most common and available way to praise and celebrate. Most worship was done on their knees, bowing before the altar or standing with hands raised toward heaven.

There are many names for God such as Jehovah, the Great I Am, Creator, Jehovah Jirah, and many more that you will learn through your studies. Jesus is also known by many names; He is the King of Kings, Lord of Lords, the Lamb, the Great Shepherd, the Lion of Judah, and the Lily of the Valley. You will learn more about all the "hats" Jesus wears.

What Is Glory?

Glory in Christian circles means awesome splendor, astounding beauty, and praise and thanksgiving offered as an act of worship to God. Shekinah Glory is reserved for God and usually refers to His presence in the ark of the covenant. Some people say they are "going home to glory" meaning they are on their way to heaven. True glory is given only to God.

GIVING

What Does The Bible Say About Giving?

God is love. Through His loving nature, He blesses. In other words, He gives you special gifts. Actually, anything and everything good comes from your Father. Every breath, every heartbeat, and every life is a gift from God.

Since man was created in the image of God with His nature, man is designed to give, to share, and to bless others. Yes, giving finances is included; however, how powerful is a smile, a hug, or an encouraging word? Relationships between people can be more valuable than any other gift. Think about your best friend. No money could replace that person.

What about your parents or siblings? They are irreplaceable treasures God blessed you with. God hunted through all creation to find the exact parents that would form you into what you are today. He uses all your good experiences as well as the unpleasant ones to bring you to today. You are exactly what He wants for His plans. You are exactly where He wants you to be.

All you are and ever will be is truly a gift from your Father. He gave you life because He wanted you to be His friend, to walk with Him and talk with Him and to work with Him to reach others.

Because you are designed to be like God, you also have a giving spirit. You talk, share, communicate, interact, work with, talk with, and enjoy life with others. You find something your spouse would really like or a friend would enjoy. You love the smile on their face as they discover and appreciate your thoughtfulness and generosity. You like making other people happy.

God gave instructions regarding giving in the Bible. Everything on earth actually does belong to Him. He allows us access to use and enjoy His gifts, and as long as we follow His instructions, He continues to bless. Remember, all good things come from Him.

Where do you suppose such things as greed, possessiveness, and making material things a god come from? Not from your Father

God. Anything that draws you away from God is from the enemy. You choose. Who do you serve?

God says, "You shall not have any gods before me." Anything you place before God becomes an idol in your life.

Become sensitive to His voice. Give when and where God leads you. There are several ways to give according to scriptural principles, and God rewards.

Giving or tithing is a powerful aspect of worship. As you give in obedience, you are honoring God. You are telling God that you trust Him, love Him, and believe in Him and His Word. You appreciate what He is, Who He is, and everything that He has done for you.

Some people are always greedy for more, but the godly love to give! (Proverbs 21:26)

Do I Have to Tithe?

Tithing is found throughout the Bible. It simply means returning 10 percent of your increase to God. He leaves 90 percent for you to live on. Ten percent doesn't seem like much; however, the greedy and worldly man thinks that is a fortune. If you were an actress or a sports figure today, you would have an agent who would require 10, 15, or 20 percent of all your earnings. You wouldn't argue because your contract would itemize the details you agreed on.

Likewise, God has a powerful contract with you: His Word. You accepted His contract at salvation. The contract says you will return 10 percent of your increase to Him. Even though you may forget, He never breaks or forgets His Word. He blesses even when He is ignored.

Malachi 3:10–12 is one of the most used texts of the Bible regarding tithing or giving to God. Pay attention to every word. The entire message is very important.

"Bring all the tithes into the storehouse so there will be enough food in my Temple. If you do," says the Lord of Heaven's Armies, "I will open the windows of heaven for you. I will pour out a blessing so great you won't have enough room to take it in! Try it! Put me to the test! Your crops will be abundant, for I will guard them from insects and disease. Your grapes will not fall from the vine before they are ripe," says the Lord of Heaven's Armies. "Then all nations will call you blessed, for your land will be such a delight," says the Lord of Heaven's Armies. (Malachi 3:10–12)

God asks for His portion or 10 percent of your increase. This money is to pay for His work around the world. It pays the pastor who teaches, preaches, counsels, prays for, and loves on God's people, you and your family. It pays for a building for the body of Christ to gather, the air conditioning or heat for creature comfort, electricity for the lights and sound systems, chairs to sit on, a multipurpose room for dinners, and receptions or children's activities. The church then tithes with what they receive by supporting missionaries in parts of the world you would never venture into.

If you want your gifts to be thoroughly blessed and considered holy, you will obediently give God the first portion of your increase, not what is leftover.

If the part of the dough offered as firstfruits is holy, then the whole batch is holy. (Romans 11:16b, NIV)

God gave His firstfruit, Jesus, as a gift to man to die on a cruel cross for redemption and reconciliation. Man is to give his firstfruits back to God. By doing so, He makes all increase of your income holy and anointed. What does this mean? You put your faith in God and His provision. The first tenth goes directly to God before you pay any of your bills. Once God receives His portion, the rest of the money seems to pay the bills and then stretch through the rest of the month miraculously. All your income or increase then is holy, anointed, and will produce great things. Often you will find or receive extra income, which you didn't expect.

God wants His children to give with a smiling face, not a resentful frown. He allows you the privilege of giving to Him. Your gifts to Him reflect how blessed you are. Why wouldn't you smile? Helping others is a blessing in itself.

> *You must each decide in your heart how much to give. And don't give reluctantly or in response to pressure. For God loves a person who gives cheerfully.* (2 Corinthians 9:7)

God does depend on His children to be good stewards of His provision. Reckless spending can get you in trouble. Excessive credit puts you into bondage. Your choice, not God's best. Remember, consequences do come when you do it your way instead of God's way.

With obedience, He blesses you more and more. He protects you and all you own. His protection is like a huge umbrella. As long as you do it His way, you are safe and secure under the protection of His wings (umbrella). Do it your own way, and you won't be under the umbrella. You will be stepping into the enemy's territory and will quite likely get attacked. You must make the choice to stay rebellious and do it your way, or get under His umbrella of protection.

> *Keep me as the apple of Your eye; Hide me under the shadow of Your wings.* (Psalm 17:8, NKJV)

Your tithes go to your local church or the source that is feeding you (teaching, guiding, and praying for you). If you're not sure who that is, who do you call when you need prayer or counseling?

The good news is that we no longer tithe because of the law. We tithe because of love. We don't *have to* tithe, we *get to*!

What are Offerings?

There is never a limit on what you give to God or His work. Yes, there is a limit on how much you can give to church or charity according to the tax code of the country and still receive a tax deduction. However, the return you get from giving generously to God far exceeds any tax break you receive from the government.

Offerings include any amount you give over and above the tithe. Remember, tithing means you are returning 10 percent back to God. That's all He requires. Offerings may mean you give over and above the tithe to some area of His work. In return, He blesses your offerings thirty, fifty, or a hundred fold. According to Deuteronomy 1:11, He can multiply you by one thousand times.

The seed that fell on good soil represents those who truly hear and understand God's word and produce a harvest of thirty, sixty, or even a hundred times as much as had been planted! (Matthew 13:23)

When Isaac planted his crops that year, he harvested a hundred times more grain than he planted, for the Lord blessed him. (Genesis 26:12)

And may the Lord, the God of your ancestors, multiply you a thousand times more and bless you as he promised! (Deuteronomy 1:11)

Remember this—a farmer who plants only a few seeds will get a small crop. But the one who plants generously will get a generous crop. You must each decide in your heart how much to give. And don't give reluctantly or in response to pressure. "For God loves a person who gives cheerfully." And God will generously provide all you need. Then you will always have everything you need and plenty left over to share with others. (2 Corinthians 9:6–8)

What Are Alms?

Alms include anything you give to the poor or the beggar on the street. Perhaps, God prompts you to walk up to a young person and hand them money. Or you anonymously give a car to someone who desperately needs transportation. No one knows what you have done. There is no tax deduction at the end of the year. You have simply obeyed God. Your reward comes from Him.

Where Can I Find Good Ground?

A ministry or charitable organization that is doing something very positive in God's kingdom is considered "good ground" for planting your seed (your offerings). They are reaching the lost, healing the sick, and obeying God's voice as they travel the world.

Yes, church programs are great, and dinners and fun activities are necessary to maintain good fellowship amongst believers. However, to follow the Great Commission, the lost and hurting of the world have to be reached, saved, and healed.

But do not forget to do good and to share, for with such sacrifices God is well pleased. (Hebrews 13:16, NKJV)

Do not forget to entertain strangers, for by so doing some have unwittingly entertained angels. (Hebrews 13:2, NKJV)

Giving to God is fun. It is just one way to say, "Thank You, Father!" Some teach, "You give to get." That is not accurate. You can't pay God to get Him to move. However, you can remind Him of His promises. For instance, according to Malachi 3:10, you can remind Him that you have tithed and that you do expect Him to protect you and your property. You also know obedience brings blessings. Not to expect God to bless you is to deny God and call Him a liar!

Recognize His blessings. Give credit to the Giver of life and all blessings. Treasure His gifts and use them well. Just as sins are carried on for generations, your blessings will also pass on to your offspring. Your faith and faithfulness will stretch to generations after you. The blessings God gave to Abraham were endless down to all generations, which means they can never be contained. Your blessings will do the same.

Do you think God enjoys watching His children suffer? No, it is His good pleasure to give you gifts, His kingdom. You can make God happy! Plant your seed where it will reproduce and yield a great harvest.

Blessings, or your harvest, come from God. They can pass through your hands to bless others, or you can hide them in a closet. Often, God wants to bless others by using you. He will get blessings to you if He can get them through you.

The Lord was with Joseph, so he succeeded in everything he did as he served in the home of his Egyptian master. Potiphar noticed this and realized that the Lord was with Joseph, giving him success in everything he did. This pleased Potiphar, so he soon made Joseph his personal attendant. He put him in charge of his entire household and everything he owned. From the day Joseph was put in charge of his master's household and property, the Lord began to bless Potiphar's household for

Joseph's sake. All his household affairs ran smoothly, and his crops and livestock flourished. (Genesis 39:2–5)

Do you want to hang around down-in–the-mouth, depressed people who look like they are on their last leg? Your compassionate heart may want to help them, but you will not want to stay around them for long. Why would the unsaved want to be around Christians who look long-faced, appear unfriendly, and speak negatively all the time?

Blessings can come in the form of people as well as things. Be a blessing to others. Smile. Be friendly. People will be drawn to you to hear the Good News. The Christian life is fun and full of God-arranged surprises (blessings). People like to be around successful people. Why? Blessings tend to spread. They attract. Your blessings affect everyone around you.

Never seek God only for what He can provide for you. Priorities come into play again. Worship Him for Who He is. Be thankful and appreciative. Your requests should not be selfish and self-centered. Yes, you will ask for things pertaining to your situation; however, your prayers should not be focused on you and your wants all the time.

But your heavenly Father already knows all your needs. Seek the Kingdom of God above all else, and live righteously, and he will give you everything you need. So don't worry about tomorrow, for tomorrow will bring its own worries. Today's trouble is enough for today. (Matthew 6:32–34)

God said to Solomon, "Because your greatest desire is to help your people, and you did not ask for wealth, riches, fame, or even the death of your enemies or a long life, but rather you asked for wisdom and knowledge to properly govern my people—I will certainly give you the wisdom and knowledge

*you requested. But I will also give you wealth, riches, and
fame such as no other king has had before you or will ever
have in the future!"* (2 Chronicles 1:11–12)

Solomon is considered one of the wisest men who ever lived on
the earth. He is a good example for everyone to follow. He sought
God's wisdom and knowledge; however, God blessed him with
much more. Seek God first. He will give you more than you expect.

*Now to Him who is able to do exceedingly abundantly above
all that we ask or think, according to the power that works in
us, to Him be glory in the church by Christ Jesus to all generations, forever and ever. Amen.* (Ephesians 3:20–21, NKJV)

SECTION EIGHT

EVANGELISM

What Is Evangelism?

How do I share my new life with others? With much certainty, those who know you best will notice a change in you and your behavior.

Many new believers become so enthusiastic that they overpower everyone they see and want to tell all the details of their new experience. If you are filled with such enthusiasm, you may have some interesting days ahead of you.

Some people will reject you. You won't get invited to happy hour at the local pub or to the wild parties. That is a good thing because you don't need that kind of atmosphere any longer. You need to surround yourself with other believers who will encourage you to stay on the path to God's best for your life.

Family may make fun of you or ostracize you. An often-repeated comment is, "Oh, you will get over it!" Not unless you reject God and head towards hell again! Do not be conformed to the world. Hold onto God and His wisdom. God's wisdom is hidden for you and not from you. Natural man can't find God using earthly means; neither can he understand God without His Spirit.

And the Scripture was fulfilled which says, "Abraham believed God, and it was accounted to him for righteousness." And he was called the friend of God. (James 2:23, NKJV)

Adulterers and adulteresses! Do you not know that friendship with the world is enmity with God? Whoever therefore wants to be a friend of the world makes himself an enemy of God. (James 4:4, NKJV)

Without accepting Jesus, you will never understand why you were born. God has a divine purpose for every person. Only you can reach someone God has His eye on. Only you can fulfill your purpose for living. Only God knows exactly what He wants you to do.

Once you discover your purpose, your God-given assignment, the next question follows. What are you doing with it? For instance, you are a great teacher. Does God want you to teach His children? You love to sing. Are you singing for Him?

Evangelism means spreading the Good News of Jesus and Christianity to others. Yes, an evangelist practices evangelism; however, with Jesus' instruction in the Great Commission, every Christian is to go and tell others about Him. Evangelists often travel long distances. You can travel within the corners of your world and share your faith with those you come in contact with. God will use you right where you are.

Your spirit will tune in to Jesus' Spirit and opportunities will come your way. You will be connected with other Christians and make new friends. Your Christian family will often become more valuable to your existence than your earthly family.

When you tell your story of salvation to another, you are sharing your testimony. By telling someone what you "witnessed," you are sharing your personal experience with Christ. As you live your daily activities, others watch what you are saying with your actions, not your words. Your life then becomes a living "witness" to the world. You are showing the world the characteristics of Who you belong to, either God or the enemy.

But you will receive power when the Holy Spirit comes upon you. And you will be my witnesses, telling people about me everywhere—in Jerusalem, throughout Judea, in Samaria, and to the ends of the earth." (Acts 1:8)

One piece of advice as you share with others is to talk to them but listen carefully. Find out where they are spiritually. A nonbeliever won't appreciate you loading them up with ten books and hours of CDs about your new-found faith. Let them ask the questions. As their interest increases, tell them more. Give them what they can handle. Don't overwhelm them.

Everyone learns at a different rate. One may love enthusiastic encouragement. Another may need quiet one-on-one intimate discussions. Listen to what the Holy Spirit is telling you to do. There may be times when all you need to do is say, "God loves you," and then walk away.

For someone to accept Jesus and get saved, they may need many subtle hints before they really pay attention. They may have heard dozens of "God loves you" along their path until one day, their heart totally opens up to hear more. Just your calm loving presence may draw them to you. Their heart is open to hear the Good News.

Then he said to the disciples, "Anyone who accepts your message is also accepting me. And anyone who rejects you is rejecting me. And anyone who rejects me is rejecting God, who sent me." (Luke 10:16)

Don't believe that you are the only one who can witness to your family and get them ALL saved. Even Jesus' friends in His hometown didn't believe Who He was. Listen to God. Say what He tells you to say and go on your way. You aren't the one getting someone saved anyway. It is the Holy Spirit who draws them.

Look! I stand at the door and knock. If you hear my voice and open the door, I will come in, and we will share a meal together as friends. Those who are victorious will sit with me on my throne, just as I was victorious and sat with my Father on his throne. Anyone with ears to hear must listen to the Spirit and understand what he is saying to the churches. (Revelations 3:20–22)

You had to open the door to your heart and invite Him to come into your life. He couldn't open the door! He had to have your permission. The next person you talk to has to make the same decision. You can't force anyone to follow you to heaven. Rather, you share, and they listen.

For no one can come to me unless the Father who sent me draws them to me, and at the last day I will raise them up. (John 6:44)

But you, dear friends, must build each other up in your most holy faith, pray in the power of the Holy Spirit, and await the mercy of our Lord Jesus Christ, who will bring you eternal life. In this way, you will keep yourselves safe in God's love. And you must show mercy to those whose faith is wavering. Rescue others by snatching them from the flames of judgment. Show mercy to still others, but do so with great caution, hating the sins that contaminate their lives. (Jude 1:20–23)

SECTION NINE

CHURCH

Do I Have To Go To Church?

For years people believed God could only be found in a church building. But His church is actually the believers who gather to share, learn, and support one another in a structure designated as a building to house His church. Early Christians gathered in their homes. They embodied the church of that day. Many churches start in homes in today's world also. Countries that don't support Christianity force believers to meet secretly in their homes. Remember, His church is not just a building; it is the body of believers.

Why do people gather? They meet to worship God together, learn new things from the leaders, pray for one another, encourage one another, and love on one another with the love of the Lord. Believers are not all on the same spiritual level. Just like real life, there are the seniors, the adults, the teenagers, and the young in your Christian family.

Occasionally, you will encounter a teenager (in real years) with spiritual wisdom and faith that outshines that of "older" (in real years) members of the church. Conversely, when a "senior" gets saved late in life, spiritually they are babies and have to start with the basics.

The Bible talks about feeding babies "milk." After a period of growth, babies switch from "milk" to "meat." Spiritually, John 3:16 and Psalm 23 are "milk" and easy to understand. You won't stay there. You will want to progress to more complicated instructions as you mature spiritually. Find a mentor who is more mature in God's Word, not necessarily someone older than you in natural years.

You need someone to teach you the elementary truths of God's word all over again. You need milk, not solid food! (Hebrews 5:12b, NIV)

So get rid of all evil behavior. Be done with all deceit, hypoc-risy, jealousy, and all unkind speech. Like newborn babies, you must crave pure spiritual milk so that you will grow into a full experience of salvation. Cry out for this nourishment, now that you have had a taste of the Lord's kindness. (1 Peter 2:1–3)

So much of God's Word grows with you. Years into your Christian walk, a return to those basic first verses will bring a new and deeper understanding of the underlying meaning of those seemingly simple words.

Can't I Just Watch Church on TV or Online?

Having access to television teachers and preachers is awesome. Going online to watch church services live from around the world is great! For the sick and homebound, there is no other choice. However, the Bible instructs us to gather together. Don't neglect this important part of your spiritual growth.

Just like you get together with your earthly family, you need to interact and join with your spiritual family. God created man for fellowship. That means interacting with others, praying for others, learning from one another, and enjoying worship together.

You will find new friends as you join the family of believers. Often, those you meet become closer to you than your earthly family. You will pray together, cry together, and rejoice together as you grow together to be more like Christ. You will encourage one another to keep fighting the fight and not give up! Often, you will want to go more than just Sunday mornings. Church often gives you that boost to get through another few days until you can get back through those doors to hear another Word from the Lord.

This close spiritual fellowship is not available watching church services on TV or online. Use those resources as supplemental instruction and inspiration.

And let us not neglect our meeting together, as some people do, but encourage one another, especially now that the day of his return is drawing near. (Hebrews 10:25)

Which Church Should I Attend?

No one forces you to go to church. When you yearn to learn more about your heavenly family and the Trinity, one of the closest and most convenient places to go is the local church. Inquire about the churches in your area. Do you know someone who attends a church nearby? Talk to them. Research the church online for the organization's statement of faith (what they believe).

Ask questions. Is it a Bible-believing church? Do they welcome the Father, Son, and Holy Spirit? Do they teach the entire Bible? Are there classes available besides Sunday morning worship services? Do they have programs for all ages? Is there a New Believers class available? Do they have a missions program? Are they actively reaching out to the community to get people saved and into His kingdom?

Some churches do not teach the whole Bible. They choose the parts they want to follow and ignore the rest. Perhaps the messages only "tickle your ears" to make you feel good, keep you coming back again for another "boost," and urge you to give generously into the offerings. You should be excited about attending church because they will encourage you to continue the fight and build your faith. However, they should also challenge you to grow and improve—to take another step higher in your faith.

Don't feel like you should go to the first church you come to or the one right down the street. You don't have to go to the church your parents, cousins, or grandparents attended their entire lives. First of all, you have to go where God directs you to go. You will pray and ask for His direction. Visit several churches and judge for yourself. Do you feel you are getting fed? Are you learning? Are they using the Bible as a basis for their teaching? Are they talking about Jesus and the Holy Spirit, or are they using quotes from other notable men of the world? Do you want to go back often to learn more? Are they challenging you to improve and grow?

You are now a part of His body of believers, with an assignment. Only God can tell you what He wants you to do for Him. He will lead you as long as you listen and obey His direction. Your assignment will be different than your neighbor's. Basically, He has instructed everyone to "go" and "do," but how you accomplish that is individualized according to your talents and abilities.

And He said to them, "Go into all the world and preach the gospel to every creature. He who believes and is baptized will be saved; but he who does not believe will be condemned." (Mark 16:15–16, NKJV)

There are many types of churches that you can attend. You will want to understand the different denominations, and choose a church that agrees with your own beliefs. A denomination is a subgroup or religious organization made up of many church groups who follow the same rules and patterns of belief or doctrine. Member churches answer to mentors or leaders of the national headquarters. They each emphasize a certain aspect of the total Christian walk. Christian churches believe in Jesus; however, many of their rules of conduct and administration are man-made and not God-inspired. Common denominations include, but are not limited to: Baptist, Methodist, Lutheran, Church of God, or Episcopal.

An evangelical church is a Protestant church that believes in the authority of the Bible and salvation through personal acceptance of Jesus Christ as the Son of God and Savior of mankind. To evangelize means to share God's good news of the gospel and convert nonbelievers to Christianity. This includes missionaries around the world as well as anyone who wants to share their faith with another.

Pentecostal churches believe in the baptism of the Holy Spirit as told in the Scriptures. They generally fall into the group known as charismatic, which describes groups of Christians who believe in and want more of the Holy Spirit's gifts such as healing, prophecy, and speaking in tongues. The terms Pentecostal and charismatic are often interchanged. One of the most common charismatic churches is the Assembly of God.

Fundamentalist churches believe in the literal interpretation of the Bible and strict obedience and rigid adherence to the doctrine and principles of the church. They are often very intolerant of other views and in total opposition to secularism. They don't like to mingle with those with other beliefs.

Interdenominational churches are composed of members who come from varied Christian backgrounds. You will find a mixture of many denominational experiences as you listen to their testimonies. In comparison, nondenominational churches are composed of believers who do not belong to a national organization. The government of the church is made of local members. Often, they have outside mentors or overseers to call on for advice and direction.

What Is Legalism?

Legalism is common in some churches. One church may demand all laws be followed for salvation to occur. The next denomination demands the laws be followed consistently for you to maintain your salvation. Since no one can keep the laws perfectly, everyone is set up to fail. Certain foods cannot be eaten on certain days, or not at all. Fasting is not an option but a requirement, whether the person is young, old, sick or healthy.

Another group may require total holiness and judge others for not meeting their personally set standards. In some groups, for instance, to be saved a woman can't cut their hair or wear makeup, men have to cut their hair to a certain length, no one can have tattoos, and a certain level of dress is required at all church functions. Perhaps you have to talk to or witness to a specific number of people every day or you lose your spiritual position with God. This is also called "salvation by works." You have to "work" your way to heaven. Scripture plainly refutes this legalistic doctrine. This is sometimes called "dead works" because you can't "work" for life in Christ.

But people are counted as righteous, not because of their work, but because of their faith in God who forgives sinners.
(Romans 4:5)

I do not treat the grace of God as meaningless. For if keeping the law could make us right with God, then there was no need for Christ to die. (Galatians 2:21)

So we are made right with God through faith and not by obeying the law. (Romans 3:28)

Not a single person on earth is always good and never sins.
(Ecclesiastes 7:20)

God saved you by his Grace when you believed. And you can't take credit for this; it is a gift from God. Salvation is not a reward for the good things we have done, so none of us can boast about it. (Ephesians 2:8–9)

For the person who keeps all of the laws except one is as guilty as a person who has broken all of God's laws. (James 2:1)

People are sometimes judged harshly and ostracized because of previous behaviors, which have already been forgiven by God. Some people aren't so accepting or forgiving. They believe ALL prostitutes go to hell and certainly ALL homosexuals go to hell, regardless of their current spiritual condition or position.

One church denied promotion of an outstanding member of the church to the position of elder because his wife had had an annulment of a two-week marriage in her youth. Since she had had "two" marriages, her husband wasn't eligible. However, the hierarchy admitted there was no rule against an elder having a previous history of murder. These are man's self-appointed rules, not God's.

Maintaining high moral values and behavior is very important, but man cannot succeed at being perfect. As much as man desires to be like Jesus, only the Son of God ever reached that impossible pinnacle of behavior.

Accept other believers who are weak in faith, and don't argue with them about what they think is right or wrong. For instance, one person believes it's all right to eat anything. But another believer with a sensitive conscience will eat only vegetables. Those who feel free to eat anything must not look down on those who don't. And those who don't eat certain foods must not condemn those who do, for God has accepted them. (Romans 14:1–3)

What Is Liberalism?

Liberalism is the other end of the spectrum. Anything is acceptable within these church groups. There are few restrictions on behavior of any kind. This is where the homosexual community stands. They believe God loves them so much that He would never ask them to conform to His laws and precepts. They don't have to confess their sins regardless of what they do.

> *Don't you realize that those who do wrong will not inherit the Kingdom of God? Don't fool yourselves. Those who indulge in sexual sin, or who worship idols, or commit adultery, or are male prostitutes, or practice homosexuality, or are thieves, or greedy people, or drunkards, or are abusive, or cheat people— none of these will inherit the Kingdom of God.*
> (1 Corinthians 6:9–10)

> *For the law was not intended for people who do what is right. It is for people who are lawless and rebellious, who are ungodly and sinful, who consider nothing sacred and defile what is holy, who kill their father or mother or commit other murders. The law is for people who are sexually immoral, or who practice homosexuality, or are slave traders, liars, promise breakers, or who do anything else that contradicts the wholesome teaching that comes from the glorious Good News entrusted to me by our blessed God.* (1 Timothy 1:9–11)

> *Therefore judge nothing before the time, until the Lord comes, who will both bring to light the hidden things of darkness and reveal the counsels of the hearts. Then each one's praise will come from God.* (1 Corinthians 4:5, NKJV)

I am not telling you to judge people. God loves *all* people, but He hates their sin. You are instructed to do the same. You answer to God for your own actions and reactions. Align yourself with Christian groups who believe the entire Word of God and will encourage you to be more like Jesus, not like the world that is blind to the deception of the enemy. The Holy Spirit has to open their eyes, just like He did yours and mine, to the unlawful things we participated in before salvation.

What Does It Mean to Be Dedicated, Rededicated, or Committed?

If something is dedicated, it is set apart for a particular use. In church, one dedicates his or her life to God or a young child is dedicated to God. In the case of a young child, the parents and godparents are making a promise to God to raise the child with godly principles and education until the age of accountability.

At some time in the past some people have dedicated themselves to God. Along life's bumps and scrapes, they listened to wrong voices and drifted away from God. They are now *rededicating* themselves; they are dedicating their lives to God again.

People make a commitment, a determination, in their hearts, and it is often in public. Where the church is concerned, the person is committing to a promise—a promise to God or to a specific assignment within the body of Christ. Recommitment means they are repeating their original promise.

What Is Revival?

The term *revive* means to bring back to life. In the church, *revival* means bringing the church back to life by a renewed interest in reaching the lost with the good news of salvation and supernatural healing. This usually means a series of meetings, possibly with a traveling evangelist who has a very strong influence on salvation of the lost. Everyone is encouraged to invite everyone they know.

SECTION TEN

THE BRIDE OF CHRIST

What Is The Bride of Christ?

"Haven't you read the Scriptures?" Jesus replied. "They record that from the beginning 'God made them male and female.'" And he said, "This explains why a man leaves his father and mother and is joined to his wife, and the two are united into one. Since they are no longer two but one, let no one split apart what God has joined together." (Matthew 19:4–6)

God designed marriage. It is a holy union of one male and one female. Eve was originally made from a rib from Adam's side. Each individual has unique characteristics as well as functions. Together they make a whole.

Marriage on the earth is to be a picture of the ultimate marriage of Jesus with His bride. The Bride of Christ is the church. Together they are united as one. Together they are whole. Each part has its own characteristics and function. The responsibilities, requirements, and duties are all outlined in the Bible.

The man who finds a wife finds a treasure, and he receives favor from the Lord. (Proverbs 18:22)

Drink water from your own well—share your love only with your wife. (Proverbs 5:15)

In the same way, husbands ought to love their wives as they love their own bodies. For a man who loves his wife actually shows love for himself. (Ephesians 5:28)

In the same way, you wives must accept the authority of your husbands. (1 Peter 3:1)

And though a man might prevail against him who is alone, two will withstand him. A threefold cord is not quickly broken. (Ecclesiastes 4:12, Amplified)

A person standing alone can be attacked and defeated, but two can stand back-to-back and conquer. Three are even better, for a triple-braided cord is not easily broken. (Ecclesiastes 4:12)

Only an agreement with God is stronger than the agreement within a marriage. Even with God in the middle of a marriage, if one spouse is going left while the other is going right, there is no strength. Unity or agreement is necessary for success. Standing together in unity and agreement is powerful.

Finally, all of you should be of one mind. Sympathize with each other. Love each other as brothers and sisters. Be tenderhearted, and keep a humble attitude. Don't repay evil for evil. Don't retaliate with insults when people insult you. Instead, pay them back with a blessing. That is what God has called you to do, and he will bless you for it. For the Scriptures say, "If you want to enjoy life and see many happy days, keep your tongue from speaking evil and your lips from telling lies." Turn away from evil and do good. Search for peace, and work to maintain it. The eyes of the Lord watch over those who do right, and his ears are open to their prayers. (1 Peter 3:8–12)

If a couple wants God's blessings on their union, they must follow God's outline for marriage. Can you imagine Jesus and His church acting like some married folk do? The church of today is not prepared for marriage to Christ. Unfortunately, the church doesn't understand the relationship necessary for the Marriage Supper of the Lamb, which is scheduled after the marriage of Jesus to His church.

Man has been placed as the leader of the home. He is to lead as God leads him. He is also called the priest of the home because he is to be the spiritual leader of his family. This is a serious responsibility many men don't realize or accept. A husband and father is to seek God for wisdom and guidance and, in turn, lead his spouse and family to be more like Jesus. The marriage between man and woman is to look like the marriage between Jesus and His church.

For you are a chosen people. You are royal priests, a holy nation, God's very own possession. As a result, you can show others the goodness of God, for he called you out of the darkness into his wonderful light. "Once you had no identity as a people; now you are God's people. Once you received no mercy; now you have received God's mercy." (1 Peter 2:8–10)

A wife is to look to her husband for guidance, love, protection, and instruction, a husband she can see and touch and listen to. The husband has to plug into God for his guidance and instruction, a holy God whom he can't see or touch. A wife may answer to her husband and follow his lead, but a husband has to answer to God. This is quite a responsibility for a man because he has to choose to follow God in total obedience.

In the same way, you husbands must give honor to your wives. Treat your wife with understanding as you live together. She may be weaker than you are, but she is your equal partner in God's gift of new life. Treat her as you should so your prayers will not be hindered. (1 Peter 3:7)

Peter was directing that Scripture to the man of the house. If he is not treating his wife as God instructs, his prayers will not be effective. If the man is not following God, his spouse has no responsibility to follow him. He could lead her into sin.

Since Jesus lives within every believer, do you look at your spouse and see Jesus? Would you treat Him poorly? Would you be rude or impatient with Him? When any negative words are aimed at a spouse, you are mistreating the King of Kings and Lord of Lords who lives within that person. Each negative experience or feeling that occurs between two people God put together is from the enemy. Satan wants to divide, conquer, and destroy the most powerful union God created on the earth, the marriage of husband and wife.

Give honor to marriage, and remain faithful to one another in marriage. God will surely judge people who are immoral and those who commit adultery. (Hebrews 13:4)

The family unit is also under attack. If two people standing together are powerful, how much stronger is a family fighting together! God is always your first priority with your family as a very close second. A strong united family is very important to God.

Unfortunately, humans don't always agree with God's perfect plan for the family. He has left instructions for the rebellious spirit of man who can't follow His instructions.

If a Christian man has a wife who is not a believer and she is willing to continue living with him, he must not leave her. And if a Christian woman has a husband who is not a believer and he is willing to continue living with her, she must not leave him. For the Christian wife brings holiness to her marriage, and the Christian husband brings holiness to his marriage. Otherwise, your children would not be holy, but now they are holy. But if the unbeliever departs, let him depart; a brother or a sister is not under bondage in such cases. But God has called us to peace. (1 Corinthians 7:12–15, NLV)

God did make provision for divorce; however, it is not His plan for any marriage to end in this manner. Every avenue for reconciliation should be researched before ending a marriage.

Some Pharisees came and tested him by asking, "Is it lawful for a man to divorce his wife?" "What did Moses command you?" he replied. They said, "Moses permitted a man to write a certificate of divorce and send her away." "It was because your hearts were hard that Moses wrote you this law," Jesus replied. (Mark 10:2–5, NIV)

Jesus replied, "Moses permitted divorce only as a concession to your hard hearts, but it was not what God had originally intended. And I tell you this, whoever divorces his wife and marries someone else commits adultery—unless his wife has been unfaithful." (Matthew 19:8–9)

Obviously, infidelity or adultery is a legitimate cause for divorce. Too many in today's society think divorce is just a common practice and not a serious matter. Trial marriages became rather normal years ago. Couples knew if they didn't make it within two or three years, they could always be divorced and go on to another mate.

Today, people live together without even a marriage license. That is immoral behavior and is called sin. These indiscriminate relationships cause many spiritual issues.

Abusive behavior in a relationship should never be tolerated. God doesn't call anybody to be subject to the spirit of abuse. The best advice to anyone caught in that nightmare is GET OUT NOW!

The Good News still prevails no matter what is in your past, whether divorce, abuse, prostitution, homosexuality, fornication, illicit sexual encounters, adultery, divorce, or any other sin you can mention. God is waiting for you to run home to His arms! He forgives where man doesn't. He loves when man condemns. He provided a way of escape through the blood of Jesus. You won't go to hell for your sins, you will go to heaven!

SECTION ELEVEN

ETERNAL LIFE

What Is Eternal Life?

What is in your future? Since you have prayed the "Sinner's Prayer" and accepted Jesus as your Lord and Savior, you are on your way to heaven. How long will you be there? For eternity. You will live with your Father, the Son, His Holy Spirit, and all those who went to heaven before you . . . as well as all God's angels. What it looks like or will be like is one of those mysteries you will only understand when when you get there.

Yes, some people have died and returned with descriptions of glorious colors and experiences, pearly gates, streets of gold, mansions, and lambs and lions lying peacefully with one another. Only God knows what you will see or experience when you leave the earth and enter His heavenly realm. But one thing is certain, you won't be condemned to an eternity with Satan in hell. You are saved for His glory!

In the last days of the earth as we know it, the Bible describes what is called the Tribulation. The book of Revelation, the last book in the Bible, paints the picture. It doesn't take much imagination to understand the hell that will be on the earth when Satan and God have their final battle at Armageddon. Movies have been made and stories written of what man imagines it will be like. No one knows what destruction will happen during these seven years of torture, horror, and battle. Christians who have studied this period all agree on one thing. They don't want to be on the earth during this horrendous event. The one thing we can be certain of, however, is that WE WIN!

Many books and studies have been done on this subject. Many religious leaders argue endlessly to support their individual interpretation of the Scripture references. You have to study and make your own decision.

The Bible says Jesus will come back to the earth to take the church (believers) out of the earth before the end. You will hear this called "The Rapture."

What Is the Rapture?

The book of Revelation is filled with revelations from God to the Apostle John about the end of the world known as the tribulation. The exact details of the rapture (when all believers will be taken to heaven), the second coming of Jesus, and the final reign of Christ as King is a mystery and has been the subject of endless debates and discussions through the years.

Eternal life in heaven is the ultimate goal. Every person saved causes rejoicing in heaven. Jesus willingly laid down His life and died so each person born on the earth can join Him for an eternity in heaven.

Heaven and earth will pass away, but my words will by no means pass away. But of that day and hour no one knows, not even the angels of heaven, but My Father only. (Matthew 24:35–36, NKJV)

We tell you this directly from the Lord: We who are still living when the Lord returns will not meet him ahead of those who have died. For the Lord he will come down from heaven with a commanding shout, with the voice of the archangel, and with the trumpet call of God. First, the Christians who have died will rise from their graves. Then, together with them, we who are still alive and remain on the earth will be caught up in the clouds to meet the Lord in the air. Then we will be with the Lord forever. (1 Thessalonians 4:15–17)

What Are the Next Steps?

The Father, Jesus, and the Holy Spirit have given you all you need. Remember, They are walking with you every second of the day. Call on Them for your questions about anything. They are ready and more than willing to help you on your walk. Man may not be available, but They are. The more you rely on and talk to Them, the more confidence you will have making every decision of life.

This book is your kindergarten primer. You will need and want much more instruction on every subject touched on within these pages. Look for the second part of this series for more in-depth teaching and information.

You have an exciting journey ahead of you. Enjoy your new life that leads toward a new destiny. You should also remember to journal your revelations, miracles, and all the events that you experience from now on. Blessings on your walk; it will be exciting and enjoyable.

I pray that from his glorious, unlimited resources he will empower you with inner strength through his Spirit. Then Christ will make his home in your hearts as you trust in him. Your roots will grow down into God's love and keep you strong. And may you have the power to understand, as all God's people should, how wide, how long, how high, and how deep his love is. May you experience the love of Christ, though it is too great to understand fully. Then you will be made complete with all the fullness of life and power that comes from God. (Ephesians 3:16–19)

Now may the God of peace—who brought up from the dead our Lord Jesus, the great Shepherd of the sheep, and ratified an eternal covenant with his blood— May he equip you with all you need for doing his will. May he produce in you, through the power of Jesus Christ, every good thing that is pleasing to him. All glory to him forever and ever! Amen. (Hebrews 13:20–21)

SECTION TWELVE

OBEDIENCE

What Are The Blesssings For Obedience And The Curses For Disobedience?

Deuteronomy 28:

BLESSINGS FOR OBEDIENCE

1 "If you fully obey the Lord your God and carefully keep all his commands that I am giving you today, the Lord your God will set you high above all the nations of the world. 2 You will experience all these blessings if you obey the Lord your God:

3 Your towns and your fields will be blessed. 4 Your children and your crops will be blessed. The offspring of your herds and flocks will be blessed. 5 Your fruit baskets and breadboards will be blessed. 6 Wherever you go and whatever you do, you will be blessed. 7 "The Lord will conquer your enemies when they attack you. They will attack you from one direction, but they will scatter from you in seven!

8 "The Lord will guarantee a blessing on everything you do and will fill your storehouses with grain. The Lord your God will bless you in the land he is giving you.

9 "If you obey the commands of the Lord your God and walk in his ways, the Lord will establish you as his holy people as he swore he would do. 10 Then all the nations of the world will see that you are a people claimed by the Lord, and they will stand in awe of you.

11 "The Lord will give you prosperity in the land he swore to your ancestors to give you, blessing you with many children, numerous livestock, and abundant crops. 12 The Lord will send rain at the proper time from his rich treasury in the heavens and will bless all the work you do. You will lend to many nations, but you will never need to borrow from them.

13 If you listen to these commands of the Lord your God that I am giving you today, and if you carefully obey them, the Lord will make you the head and not the tail, and you will always be on top and never at the bottom. 14 You must not turn away from any of the commands I am giving you today, nor follow after other gods and worship them.

CONSEQUENCES (CURSES) FOR DISOBEDIENCE

15 "But if you refuse to listen to the Lord your God and do not obey all the commands and decrees I am giving you today, all these curses will come and overwhelm you:

16 Your towns and your fields will be cursed. 17 Your fruit baskets and breadboards will be cursed. 18 Your children and your crops will be cursed. The offspring of your herds and flocks will be cursed. 19 Wherever you go and whatever you do, you will be cursed.

20 "The Lord himself will send on you curses, confusion, and frustration in everything you do, until at last you are completely destroyed for doing evil and abandoning me. 21 The Lord will afflict you with diseases until none of you are left in the land you are about to enter and occupy. 22 The Lord will strike you with wasting diseases, fever, and inflammation, with scorching heat and drought, and with blight and mildew. These disasters will pursue you until you die.

23 *The skies above will be as unyielding as bronze, and
the earth beneath will be as hard as iron. 24 The Lord will
change the rain that falls on your land into powder, and dust
will pour down from the sky until you are destroyed.*

25 *"The Lord will cause you to be defeated by your enemies.
You will attack your enemies from one direction, but you will
scatter from them in seven! You will be an object of horror to
all the kingdoms of the earth. 26 Your corpses will be food for
all the scavenging birds and wild animals, and no one will be
there to chase them away.*

27 *"The Lord will afflict you with the boils of Egypt and
with tumors, scurvy, and the itch, from which you cannot be
cured. 28 The Lord will strike you with madness, blindness,
and panic. 29 You will grope around in broad daylight like
a blind person groping in the darkness, but you will not find
your way. You will be oppressed and robbed continually, and
no one will come to save you.*

30 *"You will be engaged to a woman, but another man will
sleep with her. You will build a house, but someone else will
live in it. You will plant a vineyard, but you will never enjoy its
fruit. 31 Your ox will be butchered before your eyes, but you will
not eat a single bite of the meat. Your donkey will be taken from
you, never to be returned. Your sheep and goats will be given to
your enemies, and no one will be there to help you. 32 You will
watch as your sons and daughters are taken away as slaves. Your
heart will break for them, but you won't be able to help them.*

33 *A foreign nation you have never heard about will eat
the crops you worked so hard to grow. You will suffer under
constant oppression and harsh treatment. 34 You will go mad*

because of all the tragedy you see around you. 35 The Lord will cover your knees and legs with incurable boils. In fact, you will be covered from head to foot.

36 "The Lord will exile you and your king to a nation unknown to you and your ancestors. There in exile you will worship gods of wood and stone! 37 You will become an object of horror, ridicule, and mockery among all the nations to which the Lord sends you.

38 "You will plant much but harvest little, for locusts will eat your crops. 39 You will plant vineyards and care for them, but you will not drink the wine or eat the grapes, for worms will destroy the vines. 40 You will grow olive trees throughout your land, but you will never use the olive oil, for the fruit will drop before it ripens. 41 You will have sons and daughters, but you will lose them, for they will be led away into captivity. 42 Swarms of insects will destroy your trees and crops.

43 "The foreigners living among you will become stronger and stronger, while you become weaker and weaker. 44 They will lend money to you, but you will not lend to them. They will be the head, and you will be the tail!

45 "If you refuse to listen to the Lord your God and to obey the commands and decrees he has given you, all these curses will pursue and overtake you until you are destroyed. 46 These horrors will serve as a sign and warning among you and your descendants forever.

47 If you do not serve the Lord your God with joy and enthusiasm for the abundant benefits you have received, 48 you will

serve your enemies whom the Lord will send against you. You will be left hungry, thirsty, naked, and lacking in everything. The Lord will put an iron yoke on your neck, oppressing you harshly until he has destroyed you.

49 "The Lord will bring a distant nation against you from the end of the earth, and it will swoop down on you like a vulture. It is a nation whose language you do not understand, 50 a fierce and heartless nation that shows no respect for the old and no pity for the young. 51 Its armies will devour your livestock and crops, and you will be destroyed. They will leave you no grain, new wine, olive oil, calves, or lambs, and you will starve to death. 52 They will attack your cities until all the fortified walls in your land—the walls you trusted to protect you—are knocked down. They will attack all the towns in the land the Lord your God has given you.

53 "The siege and terrible distress of the enemy's attack will be so severe that you will eat the flesh of your own sons and daughters, whom the Lord your God has given you. 54 The most tenderhearted man among you will have no compassion for his own brother, his beloved wife, and his surviving children. 55 He will refuse to share with them the flesh he is devouring—the flesh of one of his own children—because he has nothing else to eat during the siege and terrible distress that your enemy will inflict on all your towns.

56 The most tender and delicate woman among you—so delicate she would not so much as touch the ground with her foot—will be selfish toward the husband she loves and toward her own son or daughter. 57 She will hide from them the afterbirth and the new baby she has borne, so that she herself can secretly eat them.

187

She will have nothing else to eat during the siege and terrible distress that your enemy will inflict on all your towns.

58 "If you refuse to obey all the words of instruction that are written in this book, and if you do not fear the glorious and awesome name of the Lord your God, 59 then the Lord will overwhelm you and your children with indescribable plagues. These plagues will be intense and without relief, making you miserable and unbearably sick. 60 He will afflict you with all the diseases of Egypt that you feared so much, and you will have no relief. 61 The Lord will afflict you with every sickness and plague there is, even those not mentioned in this Book of Instruction, until you are destroyed. 62 Though you become as numerous as the stars in the sky, few of you will be left because you would not listen to the Lord your God.

63 "Just as the Lord has found great pleasure in causing you to prosper and multiply, the Lord will find pleasure in destroying you. You will be torn from the land you are about to enter and occupy. 64 For the Lord will scatter you among all the nations from one end of the earth to the other. There you will worship foreign gods that neither you nor your ancestors have known, gods made of wood and stone! 65 There among those nations you will find no peace or place to rest. And the Lord will cause your heart to tremble, your eyesight to fail, and your soul to despair. 66 Your life will constantly hang in the balance. You will live night and day in fear, unsure if you will survive.

67 In the morning you will say, 'If only it were night!' And in the evening you will say, 'If only it were morning!' For you will be terrified by the awful horrors you see around you. 68 Then the Lord will send you back to Egypt in ships, to a destination I promised you would never see again. There you will offer to sell yourselves to your enemies as slaves, but no one will buy you."

I want to encourage you to walk in obedience and the blessings that come with it.

What's Next? There Must Be More!

The two most important days of your life are the day you were born and the day you find out why! I trust this book has helped you to discover why you were born onto this earth and why you've been born again into the kingdom of God.

There is so much more for you than what I was able to share in this book. I strongly encourage you to give 100 percent of yourself to your relationship with God. Give Him everything. Give Him all of your heart, mind, soul, and strength. Nothing you ever do in this world will produce the kind of return on your investment as following these simple guidelines. Natural life starts small and develops with baby steps over months and years of learning, development, and growth. Likewise, a spiritual life of power, vitality, and love is produced by a series of small steps over a long period of time. No one becomes a giant in the Christian faith overnight.

You will become the product of all the small decisions and little investments you make. Choose the proper foundation and God, the wise Master Builder, will create in you a magnificent house for His glory and your wellbeing. Everything you need in life is found in Jesus Christ. He made you and He sustains you. He always knows what is best for you. Expect the best from Him and give your best to Him. If you do, you will never be ashamed or disappointed.

While you have received answers to common questions people have about their Christian faith, I trust you have also learned how to research what the Bible has to say and find answers for yourself.

The transition from unsaved to saved is a journey filled with revelation, excitement, and change. The Christian life is full of change. Yes, things will change. The way you look, the way you talk, the way you walk through life will change. Are you ready to take the next step to victorious Christian living?

God knew you before you were born and has great plans for your life. Are you willing to be everything God wants you to be? There is so much more.

The Lord gave me this message:
"I knew you before I formed you in your mother's womb.
Before you were born I set you apart
and appointed you as my prophet to the nations."
(Jeremiah 1:4–6)

"For I know the plans I have for you," says the Lord.
"They are plans for good and not for disaster,
to give you a future and a hope."
(Jeremiah 29:11)

www.JoanHunter.org